Vision

Vision

*The Key to Personal Destiny and
Organizational Leadership*

Pukuta N. Mwanza BMinSc, MA(RSD), MA(OrgL)

Sovereign World

Sovereign World Ltd
PO Box 784
Ellel
Lancaster LA1 9DA
United Kingdom

ISBN: 978–1–85240–464–2

Cover design by CCD, www.ccdgroup.co.uk
Typeset by CRB Associates, Reepham, Norfolk
Printed in Malta

Contents

Acknowledgments

Writing this book has been an exciting journey with much corporate effort and I wish to acknowledge all those who provided significant help and encouragement to me. Completing the project enabled me to fulfill part of my personal vision of contributing towards the equipping of the saints in their service to God.

Although I cannot list every one of those who have contributed to this process, I trust that they will know from the depth of my heart how much I have valued their support. Even if it was not specifically related to the publication of this book, their help in other areas of my life provided me with the ability and much needed time and motivation to write. I acknowledge them all as special pillars in the fulfillment of my vision.

The response and feedback from many pastors and leaders who initially listened to me teach on this subject gave me the motivation to develop it further. Also, the very encouraging comments that I obtained about my dissertation on a similar subject created a buoyant force to put this material into book form for wider use. I hope that the book will thus benefit many individuals and leaders, not just in academic settings but as a practical resource.

I express my thanks to Reverend David Becker of Emmaus Road Ministries Inc. for his encouragement and very useful comments. I greatly appreciate Susan Cuthbert for editing the manuscript as this helped to improve the text further to its current form.

I greatly appreciate the efforts of Sovereign World Ltd for funding and publishing the book that is now in your hands. More personally, I wish to sincerely thank Chris and Jan Mungeam, the directors of Sovereign World Trust, for their invaluable support and encouragement. Since my first book was published (*A Christian Attitude towards Suffering and Pain*), they have always been of great help. In addition, the publisher Paul Stanier played a very important role by continually affirming the importance of this subject in the body of Christ today. His contribution is highly appreciated.

I am grateful to Dr Wil & Jacquie Chevalier, the founding directors of Lifebranch Institute, Inc., California, for their financial contributions towards this project. My wife Maggie has been of special support and I offer her my sincere appreciation.

To all the staff at Sovereign World, I say, "Thank you!" for your great work. The literature you handle reaches and transforms thousands of people across the world, many of whom you may not be able to personally meet on this side of eternity. God richly bless you all.

I remain eternally indebted to my Lord and Savior Jesus Christ to whom I owe everything. He made it possible.

Pukuta N. Mwanza

Introduction to Vision

Vision is an essential factor in life. Individuals, organizations and nations all require vision, the ability to picture a future, desirable condition that is destined by God.

The Bible provides vital information to help every human being discover a vision for their personal life or for the organizations in which they serve. It declares that, "Where there is no vision, the people perish" (Proverbs 29:18, KJV). Even if people are physically alive, if they are ignorant of their life's purpose, ultimately they will miss a God-ordained assignment and a place in His wider plan.

Vision is essential because it provides focus to individuals regarding their long-term expectations for their lives. Without it, they may become aimless and disorganized. Those who are not guided by a clear vision tend to lack a sense of importance and urgency, and work in an uncoordinated manner. We all need a basis for determining the right direction at any particular time.

Without vision you cannot achieve anything significant in your life and ministry. You may feel frustrated and rebellious because you are not getting what you want. If you have no vision you will be unable to relate the activities you do with the end product, so are less likely to work hard to achieve things.

Without a meaningful vision, life can be unexciting; it is unfulfilling to live outside your purpose. If you lack a vision you may tend to move from one place to another, haphazardly trying to do many different things. You may start a project but never complete it, switching activities because of a sudden change of mind, hoping to find something that will work.

Leaders particularly need vision, or they will not lead others effectively. People cannot follow a leader who is going nowhere or has no sense of direction for their organization. A clear vision is needed for you to lead with authority and for others to have reason to follow you. Jesus warned us that blind leaders cannot lead blind people (Matthew 15:14). This is not referring to physical sight, but rather a lack of inner vision of where to take people.

Shared vision provides coherence and unity of purpose even in the midst of diversity, and is the basis for group harmony. Without a vision, people may easily become unfocused and misguided, misusing resources and human capital in organizations. Vision engenders a sense of conviction about the choices or decisions to be made in life. Individuals without personal vision may tend to live an aimless life of chance, relying on trial and error.

A vision can take two major forms – personal or corporate. A vision will be personal when it relates to an individual. It is corporate when it is associated with an organization, a business, a ministry, a church, a community or a nation. In either case, the same definition applies.

A direction for the future

A vision is a reflection of the future in the present. It is a brighter picture seen with the eyes of faith, of your personal future or that of your organization, ministry, society, community or nation. A vision reflects the purpose for which God created you or for which your organization was formed. It is to fulfill a specific objective in the plan of God.

A vision can also be seen as a blueprint for your future. A blueprint is an architectural drawing of what a finished building should look like. Just as a blueprint depicts the end product that the architect expects to achieve, a vision is what you see when the "building" of your life or ministry is finally completed.

A vision is the very special goal that a person or group seeks through a passionate commitment of heart and careful use of resources and opportunities. It has the effect of raising zeal, inspiring them to persevere and to make sacrifices to achieve that specific goal in life. The former Prime Minister of England, Margaret Thatcher, said that "people with a vision are distinctive in that they go on and on until their goal is obtained." James Burn comments, "So vision grips us, points us in a direction, and enables us to overcome seemingly insurmountable odds ... Only those who can see the invisible can do the impossible."[1]

Not about getting but giving

Vision has nothing to do with the aimless amassing of possessions. It is what you use those resources for that is important and that matters in the sight of God. Having a large collection of material possessions or being the wealthiest person in the world cannot be an end in itself. A godly vision is not determined by what you acquire in terms of material goods but what you achieve with those resources.

In other words, a vision is not about what you get but what you give away. It is about the change that you bring about with your resources that matters the most. You can build empires and leave behind large estates but these will only be empty, lifeless monuments if they are not linked to a divine plan for your life.

To take one example, if you are into buildings, ask yourself, what are they being used for? What positive change are those buildings bringing in the lives of the ordinary people? Are they classrooms for educating poor children or training members of the community in social projects? Are they making it possible to accommodate the homeless and disadvantaged? Acquiring resources should not be an end in itself but ultimately a means to bring blessings to others.

Having great wealth without tying it to your God-given vision is meaningless, and can even be an obstacle to fulfilling a higher goal. The Lord Jesus Christ told a rich young ruler to go, sell his possessions and give the money to the poor before coming back to follow Him (Mark 10:21).

Jesus taught that goods amassed on earth should be used for the benefit of those in need, and that we should put our trust in the Lord, not in hoarded possessions:

> Provide purses for yourselves that will not wear out, a treasure in heaven that will not be exhausted, where no thief comes near and no moth destroys. For where your treasure is, there your heart will be also.
>
> (Luke 12:33–34, NIV)

The source of vision

There are three aspects of understanding the linking relationships in any vision. In figure 1, this has been illustrated in the form of a triad. **God** is the starting point from whom both the **Vision** and the **Visionary** proceed.

Firstly, everything starts with God. God is the one who created us as individuals and who determines the ultimate purpose of our lives.

Secondly, the vision must come from God. Without His involvement, our dreams end as mere hopes, of no eternal significance or relevance to our future destiny. A godly vision will have God's blessing.

Each one of us has to understand the purpose that we were created for, as revealed by God. Jeremiah 29:11 declares that God has a good plan (that is, a favorable future condition) for every individual, and this plan is not for harm or evil. This scripture speaks of a vision for a particular person.

The Vision Triad

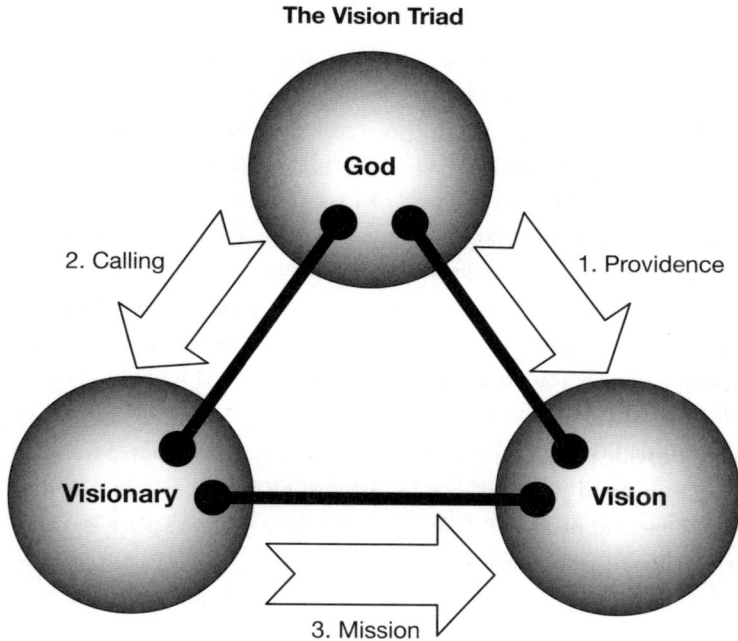

Figure 1.

God creates an assignment before He gets someone to take it on. That is why the first link in the triad is **God – Vision**. The Bible says,

> I have seen the task which God has given the sons of men with which to occupy themselves.
>
> (Ecclesiastes 3:10, NASB)

After setting the vision, God seeks an individual or corporate body to which this work will be assigned. The work comes before the worker and the vision before the visionary. This is because, in the order of God's creation, the task comes earlier than the individual or the organization to perform it.

The Bible tells us that God made the garden first and later on created Adam (the gardener) to work in it. In another passage,

God had a task and asked whom He could send when Isaiah responded. The people of Israel needed to be redeemed from their captivity in Egypt before Moses was identified and sent to help them.

Therefore, after the God – Vision link, the **God – Visionary** side follows. This involves God's calling an individual to a particular task or vision. Once identified, that person, the "visionary," has to implement the vision.

As the visionary connects with his mission we see the **Visionary – Vision** link in the illustration shown in the figure. God has a particular task to be carried out which He created you to do. Likewise, every organization should exist to accomplish divine assignments.

Are you able to define your personal or organizational vision? Do you know what you exist to achieve in line with God's wider plan for His creation?

Pursuing the vision

When God gives a vision to a person or organization, He provides the essential resources required to accomplish the given task. The Bible says,

> My God will supply all your needs according to His riches in glory in Christ Jesus.
>
> (Philippians 4:19, NASB)

However, the fact that the vision is from God does not mean that the resources will be easily accessible without any labor involved. There may be a time of asking, knocking on doors and even running to seek what is needed. As someone has said, "Even though you are pursuing God's will for your life, some doors have to be kicked in order for them to be opened."

Some doors may already be wide open for you. God told the church in Philadelphia that He had set an open door before them (Revelation 3:8). On the other hand, some doors need to be forced open; you must not passively wait for success to just happen. The Bible declares that,

> And from the days of John the Baptist until now, the kingdom of heaven suffereth violence, and the violent take it by force.
> (Matthew 11:12, KJV)

It has been said that "the only place where success is found before work is in the dictionary." Vision calls for hard work to be accomplished, which is what is meant by the Kingdom of God suffering violence. Sometimes we must engage in spiritual battle with the enemy in order to seize the resources for our vision. However, care should be taken that this violence is not reduced to physical battle and carnality. Christian battle is fought in the realm of the spirit and not in the physical.

We also read in the Bible that,

> His divine power has given us everything we need for life and godliness through our knowledge of him who called us by his own glory and goodness.
> (2 Peter 1:3, NIV)

Things that pertain to life are those that are essential for a fulfilling life, physically, socially and economically. Things that pertain to godliness are those that enable us to live a righteous life pleasing to God. Although to mobilize resources, the visionary may have to raise funds, earn money or lay up savings, the ultimate supplier of our provisions is God. The Bible adds that without Jesus Christ we can do nothing (John 15:5) and that God is the source of every good thing.

The Scriptures also declare that:

> Every good gift and every perfect gift is from above, and comes down from the Father of lights, with whom there is no variation or shadow of turning.
> (James 1:17, NKJV)

Each vision is associated with a specific place where it is to be accomplished. This was the case with Abraham: God told him to leave his homeland to go to the place that He would show him (Genesis 12:1). God could not fulfill His purpose to Abraham in his original homeland; he had to move to another place.

We also see that Joseph was made Prime Minister in Egypt where he had been sold as a slave (Psalm 105:16–19). Jonah was assigned to preach to the city of Nineveh rather than his own city, Tarshish (Jonah 1:2). Jeremiah was made a prophet to a broader sphere, the nations (Jeremiah 1:5); the list is endless.

The purpose of this book is threefold. Firstly, it is to show the importance of the vision in your personal life. Secondly, it will assist you in understanding how to walk in your vision. Thirdly, it demonstrates the link between your personal vision and the corporate vision of your organization. There is a need for complementarity between them in order for both your personal and organizational vision to succeed.

Without a vision for your personal life, you will live an empty and unsatisfying life. You need to know why you are here, and why God made you different from anyone else. You need to discover the unique purpose for which you were made. There is no greater reason to live except to fulfill the specific vision to which God has called you.

Note _____

1. Burn, James, *Fishing for the King: Building Church to Reach the Unchurched* (New Wine Press, 1997), p. 14.

CHAPTER 2

Recognizing the Vision

Everyone needs a vision of where they are going, which reveals their personal destiny. In the Bible, we see many people of vision. Here is a short list of some and the visions that motivated them:

- Joseph – *to be an influential leader*
- Moses – *to deliver Israel from captivity in Egypt*
- Solomon – *to build the tabernacle for the dwelling of God*
- Nehemiah – *to rebuild the walls of Jerusalem*
- Paul – *to spread the gospel of Jesus Christ*

Each of these examples shows the specific reasons why the visionary existed and what they eventually achieved in their lives for God. A vision is God's purpose or ultimate plan for your life. Though many people seem to die without achieving their vision, the truth is that each of them had a unique reason for being here. Each person's existence is by God's design, not by default.

What is your vision? It's by God's choice (not chance) that you were created. The issue is not whether or not there is a purpose for your life, but whether you discover it. God created this for you before you were born and you must pray to discover the specific reason that you were made.

Conceiving and birthing a vision is an integral part of realizing it. You can do this more readily if you believe that the vision already exists in the mind of God. Then it has to be revealed at a certain time and period in your life.

Since the vision is divine, it is God who is to reveal it, and He knows the most suitable season and time for making this known. The vision cannot be revealed too early or too late. It has to come just on time in order to meet all the requirements for preparation and accomplishment. By the time you discover the vision, God will have already set the roadmap for it.

> A vision is God's reason
> and ultimate plan for your life.

Once you catch the vision, it starts to illuminate your mind and heart with a strong zeal, burden, interest and commitment to accomplish it. However, take care not to adopt a wrong vision based on the lack of understanding of the will of God. It is a waste of energy and resources to try to run a race you were not enlisted to accomplish. Even if you appear to be performing well, it will bring no reward.

Imagine the frustration if you were about to cross the finishing line of a race and you discovered that you were not entered for a sprint but for a marathon. It would be too late to go back and restart the right race. You would have lost the rewards attached to your true vision or purpose in life.

Remember, no one will have a second chance after this life is over. Regardless of how attractive the visions of other people appear, stick to what is designer-made for you because that is what will provide you with fulfillment in the present, and eternal rewards at the close of the age.

Recognizing God's call

Gideon tried to prove that his calling was from God by laying a fleece before God twice (Judges 6:36–40). He tested the authenticity of the voice he had heard, asking God to show him a miraculous sign. When in doubt, seek confirmation so that you do not respond to a counterfeit call that is not really from God.

> We need to train our spiritual faculties
> to recognize the voice of God.

Sometimes what is taken as God's voice may in fact come either from our flesh or from the devil. We each need to train our spiritual faculties to recognize the voice of God and to distinguish it from other voices.

The story of the boy Samuel (1 Samuel 3:3–11) shows that God can speak with such simplicity that His voice can be mistaken for that of a human being. Samuel, clearly hearing a voice in the night, thought it was the priest Eli, yet it was God speaking. Samuel was already trained to respond to Eli's voice and didn't hesitate to go to him again and again. Because he was obedient, he found out who was actually speaking and learned to listen to God.

God's word to us does not necessarily come in a thundering voice. If we disobey simply because we think we only hear a human voice, we can miss His call.

It is possible to have false stereotypes about the way that God does things. God appeared to Moses in a fire, but this was not the case when He came to meet Elijah in 1 Kings 19:9–14. There was a fire and an earthquake but God was not in either of them. God showed up and spoke in a still small voice later on.

God can do things in an infinite variety of ways and we cannot predict how He will choose to act in our individual situation. He may deal with us today in one way and act in a very different manner in the future.

How to identify a vision

A key question is how we can come up with a vision. To a Christian, knowing our vision always comes by hearing the voice of God. Below is a list of ways by which you can discover or get to know God's vision for your life, although there are more ways by which God speaks to His people. Biblical examples are given for each case, together with the Scripture references.

Ways that God communicates to us

Dreams
- Joseph dreams about future leadership (Genesis 37:5)
- Another Joseph dreams about the conception of Jesus through Mary (Matthew 1:20–21)

Visions
- Peter sees the sheet with different species of animals (Acts 10:9–18)
- Paul sees a vision calling him to Macedonia (Acts 16:9)

An audible voice
- God speaks to Moses from the burning bush (Exodus 3:11)
- Saul of Tarsus is converted on his way to Damascus (Acts 9:4–5)
- Elijah hears God as he hides in the cave from Jezebel (1 Kings 19:9–14)
- Isaiah is called and commissioned (Isaiah 6:8)
- God calls Samuel at night (1 Samuel 3:4–11)

Prophetic utterances
- Paul and Barnabas are set apart by the Holy Spirit (Acts 13:2–3)

Inner conviction of heart
- The Spirit speaks to Peter (Acts 11:12)
- The Spirit of God forbids Paul to preach in Asia (Acts 16:6–7)

Written word of God
- Teaches, rebukes, corrects and trains (2 Timothy 3:16)
- Is a light to direct our feet (Psalm 119:105)

Godly counsel of mature believers
- Jethro advises his son-in-law Moses about leadership (Exodus 18:19)

A vision can come through a dream in the night. Of course, some dreams may be simply associated with our thoughts or experiences and should not be taken as guidance for our future. But other dreams have a destiny hooked on them and can be a channel of communication from God. It is important that we understand, interpret, and apply them rightly to our lives as we seek to identify our vision from God.

The vision to Joseph in Genesis came in the form of a dream picturing his brothers' sheaves of grain bowing to his. In a subsequent dream, he saw the moon, sun and the eleven stars bowing to him. The second dream was a confirmation of the first, shedding more light on it as it indicated that the sun and moon were his parents and the eleven stars were his brothers.

You can identify the significance of a vision by how often the themes are repeated, and what kind of passion follows them. When a dream is connected with destiny, it begins to captivate your mental and spiritual faculties. You are stuck with the idea and it doesn't leave you. You start to think and meditate along those lines. You feel driven by an urge to focus your priorities and programs on that vision.

The confirmation of a vision should be supported by God's will as revealed in His written Word – no vision should contradict the inspired Scriptures. God wants us to participate in His plan of redemption for His creation. True vision should give you joy, passion, a sense of moral responsibility and a strong commitment to carry it through. It becomes a lifeline to discover your reason for living. The importance of this cannot be overstressed; even believers can feel lost if they have no grasp of their purpose for existing.

Do not be afraid to take a risk. Getting into your vision will certainly involve risk-taking because a vision is a faith undertaking.

You will be willing to forsake everything else for the sake of a true vision. When you become "pregnant" with the vision, anything else revolves around it to ensure that the gestation period leads to a safe delivery. A vision is something that you have to carry in your heart, not just in your head. It takes your whole feeling and being to conceive and carry out.

The Bible says that it was in the heart of David to build a tabernacle for God's dwelling (1 Kings 8:17). A vision is conceived in the human heart. What captures your heart is treasure to you, so a vision should be treasured. It is that for which God made you with the characteristics that distinguish you from others. Your uniqueness is related to the vision you are meant to accomplish.

A vision may be much bigger than your current resources, qualifications or competencies. Similarly, an organization may be very small when the vision is given. The possibility of achieving a vision does not depend on your ability but on God's supernatural providence and power, and your willingness to respond. If you prepare well during the learning period, you will certainly be heading for victory and success in life. God will take care of the obstacles as He leads you to fulfill your life's vision.

> The possibility of achieving a vision does not depend on your current abilities but on God's supernatural providence and power.

The God who gives the vision will ensure that you have all that is needed to accomplish it. The resources for the vision depend not on the visionary, but on the source of the vision. He who provides the vision will also supply the resources for achieving it.

Facing doubts

Let us look at some of the biblical personalities who felt unsuitable, under-qualified or unworthy for the specific assignments that God called them to:

- Moses, looking at his own weaknesses, tried to disqualify himself from the task of redeeming the people of Israel from their bondage in Egypt:

  "But I'm not the person for a job like that!"

  (Exodus 3:11)

- Jeremiah argued that he was unfit for the role of a prophet because he was too young:

  " . . . I can't do that! I'm far too young! I'm only a youth!"

  (Jeremiah 1:6)

- Gideon felt inferior as an individual and protested the unworthiness of his tribe, clan and family when God chose him to save Israel:

  "Sir, how can I save Israel? My family is the poorest in the whole tribe of Manasseh, and I am the least thought of in the entire family!"

  (Judges 6:15)

- Joseph was only seventeen years old (Genesis 37:2) when God gave him a vision of a high-profile leadership position that would cause his family to bow before him.

  One night Joseph had a dream and promptly reported the details to his brothers, causing even deeper hatred.

  (Genesis 37:5)

- When God chose Israel as a nation to establish His name through them and to fulfill his promise made to Abraham, the nation was still very small and they were unwelcome foreigners.

  > Israel was few in number – oh, so few –
  > And merely strangers in the Promised Land.
  >
  > (1 Chronicles 16:19)

- When God told Abraham that he was going to be made a father of many nations, he had not yet had any children. Both he and his wife Sarah were very old, well past the stage of child bearing.

  > Abraham fell face down; he laughed and said to himself, "Will a son be born to a man a hundred years old? Will Sarah bear a child at the age of ninety?"
  >
  > (Genesis 17:17, NIV)

- When Mary was approached by the angel Gabriel and told that she was going to have a son, she exclaimed, "How shall these things be?" She couldn't imagine how this great task could possibly be accomplished.

  > Mary asked the angel, "But how can I have a baby? I am a virgin."
  >
  > (Luke 1:34)

- Jesus prayed in the garden of Gethsemane, asking God to take the cup of suffering away from Him when the moment of His betrayal and arrest was drawing near.

  > "My Father! If it is possible, let this cup be taken away from me. But I want your will, not mine."
  >
  > (Matthew 26:39)

Sometimes the greatest resistance and pain come just before your vision is birthed. The circumstances may be so adverse that you may feel serious doubts and fear about the legitimacy of the calling. However, pain does not mean that your vision is not in line with the will of God. In fact, struggle of some sort will inevitably follow a God-given assignment in the life of any individual or organization.

Perhaps you are now reflecting on the vision that the Lord gave you for your personal life or that of your corporate body. Your first reaction may have been to ask why God did not use someone else to achieve this task. "Why me?" "Why our ministry?" "Why our organization?" "Why our church?" These are real and common responses when you are given a task by God.

It is always humbling to consider that many in the world may be actually more qualified, adequately resourced, professionally competent, experienced or readily suited for the task. Some people feel unwilling or unready to accept God's call, but this can also show humility. It is natural to ask: "How could I do that?" when comparing our human limitations to divine assignments. Often they do not seem to match.

Looking at the calling of God, Paul wrote,

> Brothers, think of what you were when you were called. Not many of you were wise by human standards; not many were influential; not many were of noble birth. But God chose the foolish things of the world to shame the wise; God chose the weak things of the world to shame the strong. He chose the lowly things of this world and the despised things – and the things that are not – to nullify the things that are, so that no one may boast before him.
>
> (1 Corinthians 1:26–29, NIV)

It is for this reason that we can be confident in the word of God spoken to Zerubbabel:

> "Not by might, nor by power, but by my Spirit, says the Lord of heaven's armies – you will succeed because of my Spirit, though you are few and weak."
>
> (Zechariah 4:6)

We see a rather different response when we look at Isaiah. God wanted someone to send and posed a question – who shall I send, who will go for us? This missionary candidate's response was an emphatic yes. He simply said to God, "Here am I. Send me!" (Isaiah 6:8, NIV). This should not be mistaken for human overconfidence. When there is clear confirmation and conviction about a calling, it is right to say yes immediately.

The vision will be bigger than your ability

When a vision is given, the surrounding social, economic, physical or spiritual situation may well appear unpromising. Essential resources may be inadequate compared with the expected demands to accomplish the task, but do not let this cause you to doubt that the vision is a viable undertaking. The most important things are not so much what you have already achieved or acquired, although they may be a useful foundation upon which to start building the vision. Ultimately the accomplishment of the vision is a matter of faith in God, not physical sight.

The achievement of the vision can depend greatly on what you will learn from other sources. Your mentors, friends and personal experiences can all contribute effectively to the vision. It is important to learn lessons from your own mistakes as well as the mistakes and successes of others.

Sharing the vision with relevant people can help you prepare to move forward; what you lack should not hinder you from going ahead. You may need to hire the right personnel for the job and mobilize resources for the vision. If resources are lacking, instead of abandoning the project, pray to be guided by the Spirit of God to achieve the right result using different means and methods.

You do not have to be fully resourced before you can pursue a vision from God, let alone receive it. Resources follow the vision and not vice versa – you do not mobilize resources first and then decide what you will do with them. First, find the vision, and then the provisions will follow. Decide what God is calling you to do first and later find the means to achieve your work.

It is normal for the vision to be bigger than our ability, so that when the job is done, we will not get the credit for it but God will. When we have done the job well, it will not be because of us but in spite of us. It will be clear that our success resulted from God's strength, not our own. We will know that it was by the grace of God and not by personal ingenuity that we have achieved this work.

Therefore, do not formulate a vision that matches your ability or your qualifications, your experiences or resources. Pray that God reveals to your heart something bigger than you can handle so that you will have to apply faith and stretch yourself to take hold of the promise.

CHAPTER 3

Sharing the Vision Corporately

The modern idea that only one person (the leader) has the vision and the rest are mere workers to achieve it does not find a place in biblical teaching or social development practice. Each individual should be respected as having a personal destiny according to the design of God. When another person bearing a different vision solicits for support, this should be seen in terms of possible partnerships based on the compatibility between the two visions.

For this reason, I argue that a person should not be employed in an organization if their personal vision does not agree with the overall vision of the organization. The worker will only be in it for the paycheck and it is likely to lead to potential conflict between the two parties in the end. For instance, it is impossible for a person who seeks to protect the lives of the unborn to work happily in an organization that promotes abortion. This will conflict with the person's moral conscience; they will be tormented to think of the unborn babies whose lives have been terminated.

No amount of money can satisfy as much as pursuing your God-given vision. People who see financial gain as the primary factor in their job will miss the ultimate call of God for their lives. The vision is more fulfilling than the financial rewards in any undertaking.

Recognizing individuals in a team

It is important to understand that visions in the body should work interdependently. No one should be forced to abandon his or her vision in order to work at another's vision but they should be complementary. Sometimes one person's vision will build on another's.

Some people misrepresent the story of Elijah and Elisha to persuade their congregation to work for the leader's vision. They claim that Elisha entered into Elijah's prophetic ministry simply because he poured water on the feet of Elijah. But the prophet's call on Elisha was given by God and it did not come upon him simply because he was Elijah's servant.

The fact that you are working closely with a prophet does not mean that you will automatically receive a prophet's calling. Spiritual call is not given by the will of man or by mere association. You may be close to a prophet, however, because there is already a seed of a prophet within you that is deposited in your heart by God. That call will prompt you to align with those of a similar calling so that they can mentor you and assist you in developing your gifts.

Elisha referred to Elijah as "father" and his time under Elijah's ministry was one of discipleship and preparation through mentoring. It was not that the gift was infused into his life as though he never had that personal call from God. There is a danger in saying that one has to support the fulfillment of another's vision and then work at one's own vision later; if you are serving another person's vision it should be an aspect of the development of your own vision.

The metaphor of the body gives a clear illustration of how the individual parts ought to work together to fulfill the normal functions of the whole body. There is no part of the body that is able to work in isolation of the other parts. The individual parts are unique but they must function in unity.

Sometimes when a person seeks to pursue his personal vision, leaders take it as a sign of rebellion. This need not be the case: any good leader should know when to recruit and when to release the people who have worked with him all along. People belong to God and not to the leader or the ministry. They should be allowed the freedom and privilege of listening to the superior voice of God and be supported in the place where God wants them to be.

Leaders should let go of the people of God and not take it negatively when they are ready to move on, as long as this is done in the right manner. In fact, leaders should be on the look-out to assist members of their congregation or organization to discover their personal call and vision. It is a leader's responsibility to help people rise to their individual heights of destiny and not to seek to hinder them because of jealousy or pride. A good leader will help people to experience a release when they have matured in their vision and not to hold them longer than necessary.

The third chapter of Ecclesiastes declares that there is a time for everything under the sun. There is a time to come and a time to go. People working together in the context of a ministry or business can pursue their destinies simultaneously in a complementary way.

Complementary destinies

Both Elisha and Joshua had their own destinies that functioned concurrently with those of their leaders. Their service was not a random coincidence but an essential partnership, allowing them to build and achieve their individual visions in accordance with the plan of God. Like a runner in a relay race, Moses had to pass the baton on to Joshua, and Elijah to Elisha. Joshua's call as a front-line leader of Israel started where Moses' ended; likewise, Elisha's call began where Elijah's ended.

Paul showed this principle when he said that, "I planted, Apollos watered" (1 Corinthians 3:6, NASB). These are two different but complementary activities. The one who plants the seed should precede the one who waters it. These two activities are connected but the order in which they are implemented cannot be reversed: watering follows the sowing. This shows how one task builds on another.

The prophet Isaiah had a special vision from God after King Uziah died (Isaiah 6:1). Some people can only realize God's purposes for them after a great leader passes on. When the tenure of a leader has ended like that of King Saul, a wise leader will give way to those who have been waiting on the sidelines for their turn. Then, with a new leader in the front, the whole game plan changes.

David could not take his place of authority in King Saul's armor, but in his own shepherd's clothing. Each leader can only be effective in his God-ordained clothing and anointing rather than being pressured to act like the predecessor. That would be putting things into reverse gear and pulling the organization backwards.

The anointing of Elijah would not have been right for Elisha, because he was going to be living in a different era from that of Elijah. In fact, he needed a greater level of anointing in order to work effectively and so he asked for double of his predecessor's anointing. There is a unique anointing or leadership style required for each era in life.

No leader should think he is indispensable. A good leader recognizes when his time is up and knows how and when to pass on the mantle to the next person without holding onto it longer than necessary. Furthermore, it has been said that a good leader prepares for his exit from the first day that he occupies a position.

It is good to add building blocks on the foundation laid by former leaders rather than to unnecessarily replace firm foundations that have already been laid.

In a corporate context, each individual or member finds his or her unique place in the bigger group and they each play their individual roles in the team. What they do individually should be seen as a major contribution to the whole.

Corporate ownership

If leaders share their views about the vision, the people form part of the planning and regular decision-making process. This is often lacking in organizations and churches which practice a top-down approach. If the people are not given an opportunity to exercise their knowledge, gifts and experiences in serving God, they will eventually lose their special abilities and talents. This may lead to division or separation.

The claim that spiritual authority is theocratic and therefore not subject to debate is unfortunately overstretched and destroys the concept of teamwork. Broad consultation is essential so that stakeholders can participate widely in the critical issues related to their corporate vision. The "one-man" role of the mediator under the Old Testament covenant has been done away with and now we have the priesthood of all believers (1 Peter 2:9).

This means that there is now no monopoly on who talks to God and to whom God listens. Leaders who claim to be God's sole representatives have a distorted understanding of the Word of God. Such leaders may want to control people, placing themselves in the position of the "man [or woman] of God" above all others. They make themselves indispensable by saying they are the only ones who can hear from God and pass His messages on to the people. This can become a recipe for error as they are no longer accountable to anyone else for advice and checks.

The fact that someone is a Christian or has a calling to ministry does not make them immune from the temptation of abusing power. Power can be a devastating weapon used to suppress or oppress others, and should always be handled with care and caution.

Sharing the vision provides an opportunity for corporate ownership of it. It is only when the vision is shared in a participatory manner that members will accept it and identify with it. David Cormack says:

Vision must be accepted by the membership and so they need
to be able to identify with the vision. This does not imply that
the vision originates with the leader or leadership. In congre-
gational structures, the vision can readily be built from bottom
up. The vision may not come from the membership, but
eventually it must come to the membership.[1]

John Perry supports this view, saying:

God never means vision to be confined to those in key
positions of leadership. Vision has to be conveyed and shared
so that others can catch the excitement of its significance and
see it come to fruition.[2]

Although in some systems for governing institutions the
members may not be part of the early planning processes,
the vision should eventually be brought to them, discussed, and
refined with them so that the final product is owned by all.
When this happens, the vision is owned not by one individual
within the leadership but by the whole institution. In this
way, the ordinary members carry the corporate vision as their
own. This guarantees support for the vision at all levels of the
organizational hierarchy.

Ideally, the vision of an organization should not be imposed
on its members but instead they should be drawn to the vision
and want to join it voluntarily. Many people become members
of organizations and churches because they are attracted by
incentives, not the vision itself. Eventually people who do not
truly identify with the vision will want to leave the organization.

Challenges to leadership

Sometimes the members of a church or organization are to
blame for viewing their leaders as superhuman, expecting them
to possess some kind of magical powers to accomplish things.
These wrong expectations can exert a lot of pressure on the

leaders, and new or upcoming leaders may be tempted to adopt an autocratic style in order to show their authority.

Traditional stereotypes of leadership can affect how people adjust to new styles of servant and democratic leadership. They may expect the leader to do the work for the people and provide answers for their problems, rather than facilitating them in exploring their own solutions to the challenges that they are facing. Unrealistic stereotyping of leaders robs people of their power to exercise their own intelligence, knowledge and wisdom. It is unfortunate if they miss the opportunity to share their experiences for the benefit of others.

A leader who leads from within is rare and yet is the real team player. Nevertheless, many people prefer a leader to set the pace and be visibly in front, to make decisions and tell them what to do, rather than consult them.

Another challenge facing leadership is that people play different or crossing roles in the community at different times. One person may provide leadership in spiritual matters but be subordinate in another setting. When people are presented with different styles of leadership by different leaders in different contexts, it confuses their understanding of how leaders should function. A Christian leader may consider a servant leadership style ideal, while other leaders may not. It is good for Christian leaders to present biblical styles of leadership in the wider community so that they exert an influence in the whole of society, not just in religious arenas.

The lure of power

In a top-down approach, leaders tend to control the process as well as the content of whatever goes on in the organization. Titles, clothing, sizes of offices, furniture, the order of seating and even gestures used in greeting leaders can all be used as symbols of power. They point to the fact that certain individuals have higher authority than anyone else in the organization. A strong emphasis on titles or status symbols tends to alienate people, hindering them from actively participating in the affairs of an organization, or even approaching their leaders.

Only when team or servant leadership is closely applied and practiced or the priesthood of the believers upheld, will the gap between leaders and people be reduced. It is preferable to use first names rather than authoritarian titles which make false distinctions between leader and follower, clergy and laity, the most important and the ordinary, the lofty and the lower, the powerful and the weaker. This can restrict freedom for service in the body of Christ and weaken fellowship.

In some countries in Africa, titles have become a big issue. Many ordinary pastors have opted to be ordained as Reverends, Apostles, Bishops and Prophets even though some only have a congregation of a few dozen. Many titles have been applied to church leaders, such as Presiding Bishop, Chief Apostle, Senior Prophet, and Senior Pastor, or even a combination of two or more such titles for one person. Some fight to be awarded honorary doctorates although their training and educational attainment would not warrant such academic distinctions. This is because they view titles as status symbols and an important measure of greatness. This is not necessary at all.

Some pastors categorically proclaim that there is no equality in heaven and therefore there cannot be equality on earth. They argue that because there are ranks among the angels, there should be a parallel system of rank and file between leaders and congregations, insisting that God does not work through a committee but rather through individuals, or "set men." Yet the New Testament talks of plurality of leadership in the five-fold ministry offices of apostles, prophets, evangelists, teachers and pastors (Ephesians 4:11).

Even in the Old Testament, there were prophets, priests and kings; one person never did everything. When Moses worked alone to attend to the needs of all the people of Israel, it was clear that he was inefficient and doomed to fail until he heeded

Jethro's advice to delegate his authority to others (Exodus 18:14–26).

In some churches today, pastors are being attended by a team of ushers as well as bodyguards for their security. Someone will carry the preacher's Bible to the pulpit and stand by to assist them with such simple things that the preacher can do on his own. Such leaders have allowed themselves to be elevated way above what the Bible talks about.

Biblical leadership is servanthood, not being served. Some churches make a show of foot washing and yet fail to exercise true servanthood in daily ministry, so reducing the act to a mere public relations exercise. When Christ demonstrated this at the Last Supper, it was to emphasize what He had already been acting out in practice.

The standards of the world have unfortunately infiltrated the Church of Jesus Christ and we are failing to offer the lost an alternative example of biblical leadership. It is alien to teach leadership principles to the world that we do not practice. A false gap between leaders and followers creates an unhealthy relationship between them.

The craving for titles and honor is exactly the problem that Jesus was seeking to address when He urged His disciples not to be addressed as "fathers" (Matthew 23:9). In many African churches the pastors are addressed as "father" and the pastor's wife is addressed as "mother." Kevin Conner calls these "flattering titles,"[3] saying that they offer leaders "titular power" which "belongs to the spirit of the world,"[4] rather than servant leadership.

Authoritarian elements are still evident at various levels of leadership. Some leaders believe that to be effective they have to show their authority in their mode of decision-making. Democracy is taken for weakness and servant leadership is viewed as disempowering those in the front. To the contrary, power is neither lost in servant leadership nor weakened in democracy or in teamwork. When there are more checks and balances and leaders are made more accountable, and it spreads the responsibility for success as well as failure of corporate actions.

Studying the history of a particular group can help to identify the leadership approach they are likely to expect. In some African countries, inter-tribal wars fought between different warring groups seem to have affected the style of leadership adopted even in peacetime. Those who were involved in tribal fights tend to follow more military and autocratic methods not suited for participatory leadership. They need to be helped to understand that although top-down approaches may be used in exceptional times, leadership should generally be conducted as a democratic team effort.

Both personal and corporate

Whatever way the vision comes to an organization, once shared and accepted by the wider body of its membership, it immediately has a corporate ownership and identity. Bob Gordon defines corporate vision as a "spiritual vision that may be sourced in an individual, but which affects more than just that one person's life."[5] He says, "It is usually necessary to have a personal vision which fits into a corporate vision, because God rarely calls his servants to work for him on their own."[6]

This does not mean that an individual should abandon his personal vision in order to work at the corporate vision. The personal visions of members are small parts of the whole, giving the individual the desire to continue to stay and participate in the organization.

Remember that those who have no personal vision or whose vision is not compatible with the corporate vision will not find the motivation to make useful and meaningful contributions to the organization. They cannot personally identify and find a sense of belonging – it will be a mismatch.

The leader is only the channel of the vision; the actual implementation is the responsibility of the group. Bob Gordon says, "Here, God releases his vision to one person and then catches other people up into it so that the vision can be fulfilled."[7] So for every corporate vision, God will provide others of similar vision to help in fulfilling it. These may be primary members of the organization, beneficiaries of a philanthropic work, friends, relatives or partners who contribute to the vision through their involvement.

Like a pregnancy, the development of a vision should be monitored on a regular basis. Like midwives assisting in the delivery of a baby, these people play essential roles in ensuring that the vision comes to completion. They are important to the organization regardless of the scale and magnitude of their input. Such people can be mentors or counselors, or anyone who is willing to provide the help that is needed to realize the vision either at a personal or corporate level.

Gordon points out that, "Usually personal vision gives us our part to play within a corporate vision."[8] This means that people with a personal vision identical to or in agreement with the corporate vision are more likely to contribute positively and effectively to it. If the personal vision of the individual does not correspond to or is not compatible with the corporate vision of the organization, they are eventually bound to lose interest in the organization if no changes are made to graft them into the corporate vision. Most likely, such individuals may end up leaving the organization to join others in which they see themselves fitting well and easily.

When such people leave, they should not be regarded as rebellious or unsupportive. They need to be where they will find a sense of fulfillment and satisfaction. On matters of vision, people should be encouraged to go where they have a greater sense of belonging and where their contributions will be accepted, valued and appreciated. Organizations should only endeavor to keep people who are supporting the vision, as there is a danger that, "those who are not for us, may be against us."

The Bible warns leaders to know those that labor in their midst. If the people are not serving the interest of the organization, they may be serving others' interests, which may be very detrimental to the organization. There is no room for neutrality. In Amos 3:3, the Bible says, "Do two walk together unless they have agreed to do so?" (NIV). Harmony must be present between individuals in the work or ministry.

People over things

Effective leaders must identify with the context in which the people and the organization are operating if their strategies are to be appropriate. Although economic outcomes are important, the emphasis should be on the impact of the vision on the lives of the individual members of the organization. The question leaders should ask is, "Does this organization build its people?" It's been said that leaders should not use the people to build an organization but rather to use the organization to develop its people.

Modern community development needs to be about people, not "things." Although the people are integral in building an organization, in the process the people themselves should be built up. Any organization should contribute towards people's welfare and the achievement of their personal destinies. A Christian church or ministry should, moreover, strive to ensure that Christ is formed in the lives of its people. Jesus commanded that we make disciples (Matthew 28:19) – first winning converts and then forming them into mature believers who can in turn win and disciple others. Discipleship is a process of equipping believers to be spiritually mature followers of Jesus.

In the world, success is often measured numerically and some churches may adopt this standard instead of assessing the quality of Christian life being produced. Nowadays, success of a ministry is often measured by the size of the congregation, the annual budget, the attendance figures, the speed of growth and the socio-economic status of those attending. Leaders who calculate their successes by what they possess and not by the improvement they make in the lives of the people actually miss the mark. This does not mean that numbers are not important, but we need to value things rightly. Both quality and quantity count, but quality is to be valued over quantity.

Some leaders rate their ministry success by such worldly factors as how often they have flown out of the country, the price of their designer suits, the model of their cars, the size of their homes and the number of digits of their paycheck, etc. Some boast about how close they are to some "powerful," internationally recognized clergy. Little do they know that real worth and wealth is not in what money can buy.

Our true success is to do with the faithfulness by which we pursue our God-given vision. We will be judged by whether or not we have done what we were made for, not by what we have acquired unless it was in obedience to God. We can be close to some great Christian leaders and yet still be very far from the Lord – the Chief Shepherd. It is following Christ that will bring real change in the lives of the leaders and in people. In fact, it is important to always link our possessions to our vision. They should be treated as resources for the ultimate goal of accomplishing the vision.

Recognizing teamwork

Teamwork is encouraged throughout the Scriptures. A team is built from the complementary talents, gifts and abilities of its members working together, so when the team achieves its goal, its members should be commended together. Shared responsibilities in implementing the vision should result in shared benefits when success is achieved. Yet the appreciation and recognition often goes only to the leader rather than the team that worked together to bring about the good result. If team members are not recognized for their effort, they feel used rather than useful.

People reach their peak performance when they are appreciated, affirmed and acknowledged, whether their role is voluntary or paid. Success can be celebrated collectively, but if each person is individually recognized, it inspires a stronger sense of belonging, worth, and motivation. It is important not to imply that some of the participants played a minor role and therefore are not essential contributors to the corporate victory. Although leadership plays a critical role in achieving an organization's vision, the result is the sum total of all the efforts put in by different individuals.

Care should be taken in appreciating and recognizing individuals in an organization. When rewards are given to some, they should not be seen as promoting bias by minimizing others' contributions. The metaphor of the body in 1 Corinthians teaches that although some parts are smaller than others, they perform critical functions that help to keep the whole body working normally. Some parts are hidden and others visible, yet their importance is not based on their prominence. Each part of the body or team is of significance, although their functions may be very different from each other.

Notes

1. Cormack, David, *Change Directions: New ways forward for your life, organization and business* (Crowborough: Monarch, 1995), p. 100.
2. Perry, John, *Effective Christian Leadership* (London: Hodder and Stoughton, 1983), p. 105.
3. Conner, Kevin, *The Church in the New Testament* (Tonbridge: Sovereign World, 1982), p. 203.
4. Ibid., p. 204.
5. Gordon, Bob, *Master Builders: Developing Life and Leadership in the Body of Christ Today* (Tonbridge: Sovereign World, 1990), p. 286.
6. Ibid., p. 286.
7. Ibid., p. 9.
8. Ibid., p. 10.

Communicating the Vision

The vision must be communicated to the ordinary people who form much of the workforce of an organization. To be effective, this needs to be through a process of discussion, not "telling."

The catchword in communication is "sharing," as opposed to top-down methods of information dissemination. Sharing is mutual and provides a free atmosphere and opportunity for effective participation of all members. Top-down methods of communication, on the other hand, polarize control of power so the "followers" have to entirely depend on their leaders for direction.

The manner of communicating the vision is critical and it must be done by the leadership. Philip King emphasizes that, "unless the leader communicates the vision, he simply becomes an 'enabling eunuch'; he ought to be a captain who gives direction and not just a referee who reacts to others' initiatives."[1]

The timing is also important. Joseph immediately shared his dream with his brothers who clearly resented him for bragging. They hated him for what the dream meant as well as for how he shared it, and all the more so when the dream was repeated. Joseph needed wisdom about the right timing to share the dream with those who were going to be affected by it. The first questions he needed to ask himself were "Who do I share this vision with? When do I share it? How do I present the dream to them?"

Joseph's dream was perceived negatively by his brothers because they were to be made subjects rather than masters. A vision is a sensitive thing that must be prayerfully handled because it involves our lifelong service and pre-occupation. Carelessness in handling the details of the dream can adversely affect the amount of support one may be expected to get from other people and create unnecessary opposition.

Tom Marshall warns that "there are dangers in the premature disclosure of matters that are under serious consideration."[2] He suggests that leaders should wait until they are confident of the vision. If the leadership is still vague and unclear, it may affect the level of assimilation by the rest of the members. In fact, the leadership's credibility and integrity may be questioned if it seems that their understanding is inadequate, and they are operating by guesswork.

The depth to which the leadership knows its people is critical. This will show their likely response to specific aspects of the vision. Stewart Dinnen discourages downloading the whole vision onto people at one time, and suggests that in a voluntary organization, a vision is not likely to be immediately accepted. Instead, he says, it "should be drip-fed"[3] little by little, not suddenly imposed. This means sharing the vision in stages so that the people are able to gradually grasp and accept it.

Sharing the vision with the members

This process of sharing the vision should be done with ordinary members of the team so they can have a clear understanding of its design prior to being involved in its implementation. For very large organizations of thousands of members, the process of sharing needs to be streamlined. The mission statement can be shared in stages with smaller, manageable groups under various levels of leadership. At each stage the vision content is broken down and simplified to make it understandable.

In a church, this would be achieved by explaining the vision to the small group leaders who would in turn share the vision with their members. The contributions and comments of group members would then be communicated upwards to the senior leadership in order to be considered and potentially incorporated into the overall structure.

There should be close and regular consultation among leaders which in turn leads to similar consultation with people at the grassroots. This encourages everyone to strive towards common goals from an early stage. If a church or organization wishes to achieve great things, sharing the vision is the key to unlocking the willing commitment, support, sacrifice and unity of the members.

Participatory dialogue is most effective where followers have a mature understanding of issues and therefore can make significant, positive and meaningful contributions to the work. For voluntary organizations such as churches and community-based organizations (CBOs), and non-governmental organizations (NGOs), however, free flow of information among the primary stakeholders is crucial for transparency and accountability. Therefore, sharing of information between parties is essential regardless of the members' maturity. People will grow in their understanding of issues even if they are complicated or somewhat unclear at the start.

It is the leaders' role to ensure that their people are taught about the need to have a personal vision so that when it comes to dealing with the corporate vision, they are already aware of how it can be formulated and implemented. This process should form part of the training of people at all levels of the organization.

Effective leaders will not be too far away from the ground where the majority of the people are. It is always good to be a leader among the people rather than above the people. An African proverb says, "The one who rides the donkey does not know the ground is hot."[4] In other words, the people on the top will not know what is happening on the ground unless they step down and allow their feet to touch the ground – or ask the ones whose feet are on the ground. Leaders who cannot relate their programs to what their people are going through will be irrelevant and fail to meet either the people's individual needs or the corporate needs of the organization.

An American historian said, "If you get too far ahead of the army, your soldiers may mistake you for the enemy."[5] A general could be so distant from his troops that they would fail to recognize him and even perceive him as the opposition, causing them to resist or even kill him. Therefore, it is important that leaders are within reach of their people and lead them from within the ranks. Leaders should seek to be where the people are in order to know what they are doing.

Everyone seeing the same vision

Kouzes and Posner emphasize the importance of all those in an organization recognizing the value of the leaders' vision, if "following the leader" is to be meaningful:

> Visions seen only by the leaders are insufficient to create an organized movement or a significant change in a company. A person with no constituents is not a leader, and people will not follow until they accept a vision as their own. Leaders cannot command commitment, only inspire it.[6]

Leaders need to be able to see with the eyes of faith, but their vision needs to be packaged so that it can be easily assimilated and understood by the ordinary people. In the end, the leaders and the people all need to be able to see the same thing. If they do not see the same thing, they cannot go in the same direction.

In 2 Kings 6:16–17, we read that Elisha prayed for his servant's eyes to be opened so that he could see God's army of horses and chariots of fire defending them. Elisha had already seen this, but his servant was gripped with fear at the sight of the enemy troops until he too saw the heavenly guard. The follower needed to see what his leader had seen to rest his heart. If you are a leader, do you and your followers see the same thing?

Leaders must work to ensure that all the people under them are able to fully understand, interpret and personally own the vision. "Leadership is a team effort"[7] and the team ethos should be maintained regardless of the relative contribution of different members. No matter how dynamic or charismatic leaders are, they will achieve more if they work in a team than alone. No one person on earth is omniscient or omnipotent, only God. Teamwork should not be a mere buzz word, but a deliberate effort to draw in everyone to play their part, so they are not just recipients of the decisions of an elite group.

Sometimes certain team members tend to attract more attention and recognition than others for the same task that they have performed as a team, particularly at times of celebrating victory. When the team is not corporately acknowledged for its achievements, individual members tend to feel frustrated and discouraged. Ultimately, the affected members may opt to resign from the organization or withdraw from actively participating in the work.

Team members do not want to be treated as mere hirelings in the work of others. They want to see their part, no matter how small, being recognized in the bigger vision. In any organization, the corporate vision ought to be owned by everyone who is involved, whether on a voluntary or paid basis. Each person will want to be treated as a co-owner of the dream in some capacity.

Resisting wrong visions

In churches and religious organizations, sometimes the role and the importance of the visionary are over-spiritualized. The visionaries can take a conspicuous place on central stage, in some cases even idolized for the role that they have played in the organization. This should not be the case. The problem is often that the identity of the leader is so tied to the ministry that the two are virtually indistinguishable, and this is particularly so in some charismatic churches.

The visionary is not more important than the vision, in fact the visionary exists for the vision. The visionary may contribute only a part of the whole vision before someone else takes over to accomplish the rest. Some visionaries are pioneers but their successors are the ones who actually realize the vision.

One of the reasons why the locus of the vision must be spread to cover the members is to ensure that the glory arising from the project's fulfillment is not directed towards man but is offered to God. Any organization whose chief end is to glorify its founder rather than God will end up like Babel, in confusion and disarray.

Paul said, "Follow my example, as I follow the example of Christ" (1 Corinthians 11:1, NIV). This implies that we should follow leaders only as long as they continually follow Christ. Once leaders shift their focus away from Christ, they are lost and unless we change our direction, we are lost too.

The Catechisms declare that the chief end of man is this: "To glorify God and to enjoy him forever." There should be careful discernment that any church or organization does not substitute the glory of man for the glory of God. We are not obligated to be loyal to a leader or institution that is opposing God's will or which usurps the honor that belongs to God alone.

This kind of godly rebellion was exemplified by the three courageous Hebrew young men Shadrach, Meshach and Abednego. They stood for God and refused to obey the decree of King Nebuchadnezzar to worship the idolatrous image that he had made (Daniel 3:16–18). Also, when Peter and John were commanded to stop preaching in the name of Jesus Christ they declared:

Whether it is right in the sight of God to give heed to you rather than to God, you be the judge.

(Acts 4:19, NASB)

Firm resistance to evil, based on the fear of God, separates true followers from the hypocrites. It was the unwavering commitment of church fathers like Martin Luther, John Calvin and others in resisting corrupt papal authority that brought about teachings on justification by faith, salvation by grace and the priesthood of all believers. They resisted unscriptural practices like indulgences that were sold to church members as a condition for the forgiveness of their sins. Because of their firm stand, millions across the world have experienced the love and saving grace of God.

Notes

1. King, Philip, *Leadership Explosion* (1987), p. 136.
2. Marshall, Tom, ibid., p. 23.
3. Dinnen, Stewart, *You Can Learn to Lead: A Manual for People in Leadership* (Geanies House, Fearne, Ross-shire: Christian Focus, 1998), p. 78.
4. Holland, J. and Blackburn, J., *Whose Voice?* (Intermediate Technology Publications, 1998), p. 97.
5. Quoted by Warren Wiersbe in *On Being a Servant of God* (Baker Books, 1993), p. 84.
6. Kouzes, J. and Posner, B., *The Leadership Challenge* (San Francisco: Jossey-Bass, 1997), p. 11.
7. Ibid., p. 11.

Writing a Strategy for the Vision

A strategy is a process that is designed to reach the vision. A written strategy is very important because it details clear ways of accomplishing the vision in terms of specific objectives, resources and scheduling. It guides the visionary and the organization in how the vision should be carried out.

The strategy will identify key activities that directly or indirectly contribute to the vision being achieved. It should incorporate timelines to show how each activity fits into the overall calendar of events.

Anyone who is expected to contribute to the achievement of the vision should be invited to participate in designing the strategy (or should be clearly informed what their role will be and how they will be expected to play that role). People are often more keen to implement a strategy that they have personally contributed to formulating, as they are able to identify more closely with it.

Formulating the mission statement

Too many organizations or churches exist without ever formulating an effective and relevant mission statement. Either that, or the mission statements are articulated in such a vague and ambiguous way that they do not impart passion or a sense of commitment to anyone wanting to play a role in the organization.

A mission statement should explain the aim or purpose of an organization, providing a reason for its existence. Therefore it should be understood and agreed upon by the wider organization, ministry or the church so that the corporate vision is a unifying factor for all its members.

Sufficient consideration must be made to mobilize those who need to implement and sustain the strategy. For this reason, a SWOT analysis or an organizational audit has to be regularly done for every corporate body. The available resources need to be assessed and if gaps are identified, more resources may need to be gathered.

SWOT analysis is an important tool for assessing the strengths (S), weaknesses (W), opportunities (O) and threats (T) of an organization. If an organization is to be effective, it needs to work at building on its strengths, eliminating weaknesses, exploiting opportunities and minimizing weaknesses. Chuck Stephens illustrates SWOT analysis as shown in figure 2:

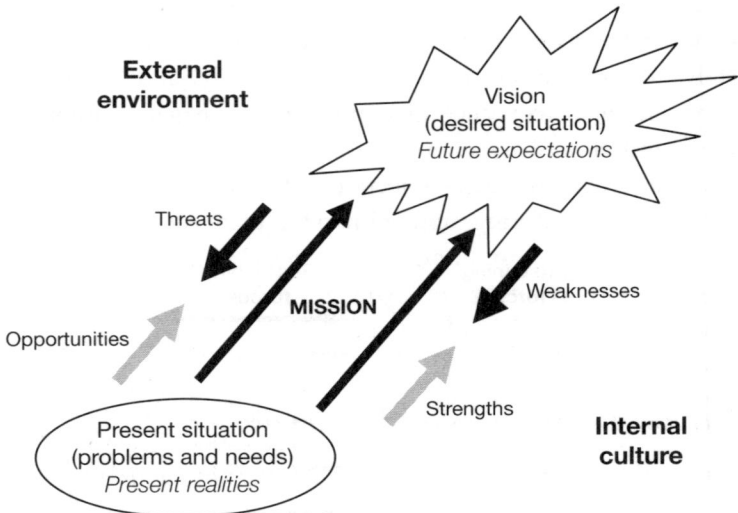

Figure 2. Source: C.O. Stephens, *Leading Groups in Civil Society*, 1999, p. 40 (my italics). Used by permission.

opportunities and strengths are shown as positive trends that enhance the achievement of the vision, and threats and weaknesses work as opposing forces against the vision of the organization.[1]

The need for a clear strategy

The vision alone is inadequate if it is not accompanied by a clear strategy to accomplish it. Any individual or organization without a written strategy for implementing its vision will lack focus in the mobilization and management of resources. A strategy will direct the most effective and sustainable use of resources.

In setting a strategy, it is important to consider the factors that may affect the vision either positively or negatively. These forces may be shown on a force field analysis (FFA) as positive or negative arrows acting in opposite directions (see figure 3). The positive arrows are the sustaining forces, enhancing and promoting the achievement of the vision, while the opposing arrows are the negative forces, resisting progress, delaying, hindering or diverting the vision from being accomplished. Through risk assessment, one can anticipate which forces are likely to be exerted in a detrimental way and therefore determine how to reduce or eliminate their negative impacts on the vision.

To deal with obstacles effectively, a disciplined process of instruction, mentoring and equipping is needed. Adequate

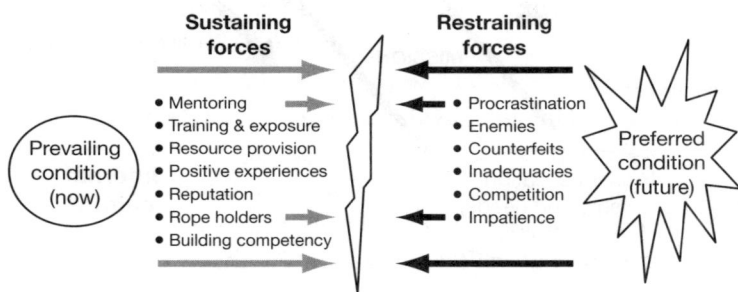

Figure 3.

training and preparation is essential for reaching the top and sustaining that position. In leadership, how you learn is as important as what you learn. This is what determines the way you respond to external pressures and threats that come along.

Corporate vision

A corporate vision is a statement about the future of a company or ministry in terms of where it is going and what it is becoming. Aubrey Malphurs defines a vision as, "clear, challenging picture of the future ... as you believe that it can and must be."[2] It must describe concisely what the organization is seeking to be. To come up with a clear vision statement, there is a need to spend a reasonable time in prayer, waiting upon the guidance of the Holy Spirit. This will provide the organization with the necessary resources and means to accomplish its vision.

A vision statement must also have a set of clear objectives that will indicate how the accomplishment of the vision will be measured. These objectives should be converted into specific, identifiable and related activities. If every activity is linked to a specific objective, it will keep you focused on what you have deemed to be important in your organization. Each activity should contribute directly or indirectly to your achievement of the vision; if it is not, it will be a waste of time, resources and labor.

Every organization needs a vision statement – without it there is lack of strategy and a major handicap in the effective implementation and review of the work. Just as there is a personal vision for an individual, there is also a corporate vision for an organization.

The vision ought to be the common factor for all those serving in an organization. David Shearman warns that, "When vision is clear but diverse, **division** results; when vision is diverse and vague the community suffers **attrition**; common but vague vision generates **frustration**. Only when the vision is both clear and common, seen and shared by all, can the community enjoy **cohesion** and togetherness."[3]

The vision statement of an organization should not be so broad and ambiguous that it fails to guide the leadership into measurable targets and specific areas of operation. The absence of a clearly defined vision means that the identity of the group is not established. Such an organization or a church may become susceptible to bad practice, to negative external influences such as strange doctrines or into doing things not directly related to the purpose of the organization.

It is dangerous for organizations to recruit front-line leaders who do not agree with the corporate vision of the organization. If they will not support it, then they may oppose it. In fact, all staff must have individual visions compatible with those of the organizations they seek to serve, otherwise their hearts and commitment will be somewhere else. A clear and well-defined mission statement should be shared with all new members wishing to join the organization.

According to Christian Leadership World web-published materials, there are six stages required to establish or to develop a vision for the organization, namely, "Preparatory Prayer, Building Blocks (important or key elements of the vision), Prayer, Drafting a vision, Sharing the vision, and Action."[4] The vision should not be established in haste. Because it must be largely prayer-based and should result from the leading of the Holy Spirit, it will be a reflection of the will of God for the organization.

By this process, members are given an opportunity to contribute to the development of a vision, engendering a sense of ownership and corporate identity. The general member-ship of the organization can provide vital prayer support as the leaders seek the face of God for the vision from the initial stage throughout its development.

Sharing the vision implies dialogue, consultation and discus-sion so that there is input from the grassroots prior to action or implementation. A purely top-down approach to information dissemination is ineffective and robs people of the opportunity to make relevant contributions to their organization.

> The process of seeking a corporate vision should be shared with the members through dialogue and consultation, not a top-down approach.

The compatibility between an individual's personal vision and that of the organization they are part of is of extreme importance. As members work at fulfilling the corporate vision, their own individual vision will also be accomplished. This is why the vision for the organization must be clearly shared to the members so that they are able to willingly buy into it. The right atmosphere is required, as Tom Marshall states:

> In order for people to contribute positively and freely in the design and implementation of the vision, they need to ... know that their leaders will respect their opinions, and will not hold it against them if they do not agree with the leader's views. In other words, there must be an atmosphere of trust between the people and the leader, if the ordinary people have to be effectively involved in the vision of the organization.[5]

Lack of trust may breed suspicion and potential misunderstanding between the leaders and the people, which will in turn affect the accomplishment of the vision. Split vision or division becomes inevitable. However, when the organizational vision is clear, it will naturally attract certain types of people who desire to grow their own visions in the context of that corporate vision.

The vision is a translation from the current position to the final position of an individual's or organization's destiny. This movement needs to take into account the following aspects:

- The strategy for most effectively and efficiently achieving the vision
- Essential resources and character qualities such as discipline and personal integrity
- The full "gestation period" required from the time that the vision is revealed to its full realization
- Systems that ensure the long-term sustainability of the vision, e.g. monitoring and evaluation

The strategy needs to determine measurable objectives, scheduling activities for each objective, and allocating personnel and material resources for each activity. This process is a vital part of preparation. A strategy should answer the questions "How?" (what process), "Who?" (what human capital requirements), "When?" (what time scale for various activities) and "How much?" (What cost).

Lack of a clear implementation strategy is a major handicap because any vision must be monitored periodically to check on its progress towards the anticipated result. Without a strategy, there is no way of knowing what means, resources and processes are needed to achieve the vision. The strategy should indicate when certain activities should be implemented in order to enhance coordination among various sectors of the organization.

Some Christians who fail to plan hide behind the "leading of the Spirit," but the result is often haphazard. The failure is not of the Holy Spirit but purely human negligence. With every vision, there is human as well as divine responsibility. A vision statement alone will not show what the organization needs to do to be unique and different from others. The strategy is the methodology of achieving the vision.

Members' involvement in formulating the strategy

The leadership should formulate a clear strategy that should be understood by the whole organization. Every effort should be made to ensure that there is wide consultation with the members on the formulation of the strategy and the process of implementing it. In many organizations including religious groups, the leadership rarely consults ordinary members. This tends to isolate the people from the core process of decision-making.

Remember that when ordinary people take part in formulating the strategy, they do not have to ask why they are doing certain activities later on. They will already have anticipated the sacrifices that may be necessary to achieve the vision and what resources need to be mobilized in order to reach the goal.

For the vision to be accomplished there must be a clear plan of how individual members will play their part in various activities. An effective human resources strategy will determine the kind of personnel to attract and recruit; it will assess the qualifications, skills and experience needed to perform various tasks.

Initially the leadership should formulate a draft of the strategy. In churches, this document should then be shared and discussed with the various groups of leaders such as deacons, ministry leaders and home group leaders; in the case of other organizations this means sharing the vision with all levels of management. When all these have provided their input and are clear about the strategy, then the leaders should share with the members of the organization during regular meetings or special gatherings called to deal with these issues.

This process ensures that by the time the vision and strategy are presented to the grassroots members, the leaders will have already owned the vision. At every stage of sharing the strategy with the various groups, it will be further refined. Vital adjustments can be made through the contributions of different members, this enhancing the implementation of the strategy.

Success depends more than anything on the members' committed involvement, regardless of how much external support is mobilized. The hearts of members must be won first before those of outsiders. Without their cooperation, resources alone cannot be of significant value to the organization. Success depends on local team cohesion and unity.

A consultative approach to decision-making can provide a forum in which all members of a team may determine the most effective ways of accomplishing their vision objectives. The leaders can discover the resources and knowledge available from within its membership, whose expertise might otherwise remain untapped. Members may donate their expertise, time, finances or other resources which may significantly cut down on the time and cost of the resources needing to be mobilized from outside.

The leadership of any organization needs to draw members into making constructive contributions towards key decisions. Some of the members may possess valuable professional expertise that is not available in the leadership. After all, there are normally far more members than leaders.

Members will be more keenly interested in implementing the vision if by doing so, they are achieving their own personal visions as well. Often a secretive approach by leaders robs members of realizing their full potential. They may seek to control information so that they can be seen as the ones in charge and indispensable to the organization. Knowledge is power and those who are not well-informed end up disempowered and unable to work well. This situation is not honoring to God.

Members' involvement in implementing the strategy

The members of an organization do not just have to approve of the vision, but to support it by performing specific activities. There is also room for people outside the organization who can contribute by material donations, moral or prayer support. Clear objectives help people with certain skills and resources to willingly avail themselves to achieving the vision of the organization.

The primary resource in achieving the vision of any group is its people, not finances and materials as are often assumed.

Leadership should work at ensuring that its members passion-
ately catch and carry the vision of the organization, by widely
sharing the ownership of the ministry.

If the members are to be effectively involved in the vision,
they should be fully aware of the objectives and how they will
be implemented. Their roles should be clearly spelled out so
that each person or task force is held accountable for their
assigned responsibilities. Of course, people will be most
productive and motivated if they are assigned tasks that relate
specifically to their skills and levels of competence.

Sometimes leaders sideline some of the most skilled persons
in their organization because they perceive them as a threat to
their job security, position or status. The truth is that no one
person has a monopoly on talent or wisdom; there will always
be someone else who can do the same task more effectively and
more efficiently. Good leaders, however, should be able to pool
resources and skills together for the common good of the
organization without regard to their own pride. An effective
leader can work with others of even higher qualifications
without feeling threatened or insecure.

Reviews of the strategy

A good strategy provides for periodical reviews on various
activities to ensure that whatever is being done is in fact
contributing directly or indirectly to the accomplishment of
the vision. Without this, activities and resources may be
wasted, as they may not be linked to the vision.

The goal can only be reached if there is a plan of everything
that needs to be done to realize the vision. The end will
determine how you start and proceed. The strategy will also
indicate when certain types of resources will be required for
the activities that should clearly relate to the objectives of the
organization.

The objectives in an effective strategy are measurable,
realistic and attainable, specifying expected outputs at particular

points. When monitoring progress on the work, they can be used to assess what has been achieved and to what extent. During periodic reviews, the operations of the organization should be evaluated in relation to the mission statements.

Any institution should incorporate an evaluation plan in its plans. Evaluation is the process of critically assessing how activities relate to the achievement of the vision; the output should always be related to the predetermined objectives. For this to be effective there should be measurable indicators set at certain intervals.

Annual evaluations should be timed so that the outcome can be shared with the wider membership at the Annual General Meeting. In-depth assessments should also be scheduled to coincide with strategic planning exercises.

To be objective, the evaluation team should include leaders as well as ordinary members of the organization. It should also involve external evaluators. A strong team needs to be multi-disciplinary so that it is enriched by knowledge and experiences of people with various areas of expertise. Important lessons learnt from the evaluation should be shared with the organization so that new strategies can be developed to enhance growth.

Notes

1. Stephens, C.O., *Leading Groups in Civil Society*, Book 1 (White River, 1999), p. 40.
2. Malphurs, Aubrey, *Strategic Planning: A New Model for Organization and Ministry Leaders* (Grand Rapids: Baker Books, 2001), p. 140.
3. Shearman, David, *Born to Win* (Tonbridge: Sovereign World, 1999), p. 60.
4. Christian Leadership World, www.teal.org.uk/vl/v14proc.html, Internet, accessed 18 September 2003.
5. Marshall, Tom, *Understanding Leadership* (Tonbridge: Sovereign World, 1991), p. 23.

Characteristics of a Vision

6

Vision and mission are not exactly the same. There is a distinction between the two, even though the words may often be used interchangeably.

A vision is about your life's journey to a desirable future position, what God says you or your organization should become. A vision explains where you are going, why you exist, and what makes you distinct from anyone else. In short, a vision is the picture of yourself or your organization that you see with the eyes of faith.

A mission statement, however, describes what or your organization does for its existence. In formulating it, you need to address certain questions to comprehensively describe your organization or your personal life. These are:

- For what purpose do we exist?
- Who is the target group that we want to reach? Who are our clients, beneficiaries, or customers?
- What service or products will we provide to that group and by what process will they be delivered?
- What change do we hope to bring into the lives of the people we are serving?

The groups of people that you want to reach – workers, members, supporters, partnerships and sponsors – will usually respond positively when they can identify with something in the mission statement or vision.

The contrast of vision and mission

Remember the unique characteristics of vision and mission:

- Vision describes your destination, while mission describes your direction.
- Vision tells where you are going, while the mission speaks of what you do to get there.
- Vision describes what you exist to do, while mission describes what you do for your existence.
- Vision is your end, while mission is the journey of life.
- Vision is purpose for your living, while mission is living for your purpose.
- Vision describes the purpose of your life, while mission describes the process to achieve it.
- Vision is about where you are going in relation to what you are doing, while mission is what you are doing in relation to where you are going.
- Vision is what you see by faith, while mission is what you do based on that faith.
- Vision describes your final identity, while mission is your current service that builds your identity.
- Vision pictures your future, while mission produces it.

The eight characteristics of vision

A vision must have the vital ingredients that lead to a purpose-led, goal-centered and orderly life that will be meaningful, satisfying and fulfilling. A vision should have the following eight characteristics:

- *Prayer-based* – it should be a God-given dream for a favorable future

- *Precise* – it must be specific enough to guide its implementation
- *Prospective* – it should point to the future, possibly far beyond the present
- *Participatory* – other people must be involved in design and implementation
- *Personalized or particular* – it should be specific to the person or organization
- *Practical* – it has to be feasible and lead to tangible results
- *Passion-inspiring* – it must motivate the visionary and others
- *Published* – it should be written down for distribution, reference and revision

Prayer-based

A vision should come out of a background of prayer, seeking the face of God. If it is given by God, the resources to accomplish it will come by the same source. He who gives the vision will also supply the provisions and protection for it. God will back up your vision if it originates in Him.

Security for your personal life and sustainability for your organization will all come from God. "If God is for us, who can be against us?" (Romans 8:31, NIV). Prayer must undergird everything that you do in the process of working at your vision, not only giving birth to the vision but sustaining it.

> He who gives the vision
> will also supply the provisions to achieve it.

Precise

A vision statement should be specific, accurate and clear. It must be differentiated from those visions of other people or organizations. Because no two people are the same, visions may be similar but not exactly the same. They can differ in terms of their nature, scope, timing or location.

Bear in mind that whether your vision is personal or corporate, you won't be alone in implementing it. Other people will get involved in some way, so make it easier for them to understand your vision by being precise, with a strategy that is clearly stated and easy to understand and follow. It should not be vague or confusing in its phraseology, or it will mislead people. To build up a clear vision statement, you may require key words. This may take time to ensure that they fit into what you believe is God's purpose for you.

"SMART" is a common acronym used in designing clear goals and objectives for programs. This acronym is built from the first letters of the words **S**pecific, **M**easurable, **A**chievable, **R**ealistic and **T**ime.

Note the important dimension of the time frame in achieving the vision. As far as possible, you should plan to achieve milestones at specified times rather than leaving this open-ended. Timed reviews of progress and performance will provide opportunities to alter plans for resource mobilization, staff recruitment and human resource development. While assessing your activities you revisit the vision statements and check whether they are still relevant to the reasons for your existence or whether they need to be revised.

Read the time and seasons that you are in. God warned the children of Israel that they had stayed long enough at the mountain and it was time to break camp and move on (Deuteronomy 1:6). Beware of liking comfort to the extent that it delays your journey to fulfilling the vision.

A vision also needs a specific environment to flourish. Discover which setting is suitable for growing your vision. Don't just go to any organization, it may not work for you. Once you find the right place, you could achieve a lot and your performance may rise way above average.

Prospective

A vision needs to look forward to a better and more favorable future. It must provide people with a picture of hope. The current condition of your life does not fully determine its final condition; even if simple and small it is a foundation to build upon. It is not good to judge people based on their present appearance without a future perspective. What has God called them to become? They are still a "work in progress."

Many people have been denied opportunities because of unfavorable circumstances or their past mistakes and short-comings. However, Jesus did not reject His disciples despite their weakness and failures; He saw their future potential. Simon Peter publicly denied the Lord, and yet he became a pillar of the church from the day of Pentecost onwards.

In many firms, new employees are recruited or rejected based on what they did in their former jobs, yet their future has the potential to be very different from their past. Some may initially have been in the wrong place or are still in the learning process. They may be searching for the right environment within which their personal vision can flourish and where they can also make a meaningful contribution to the vision of the organization.

Participatory

A visionary should identify people who can be prime particip-ants in the fulfillment of the vision. Talk to them first and let them know that you need them. Allow them to share in your vision by contributing to its design, implementation and subsequent fulfillment. At the earliest stages, some people may critique the vision to ensure that it reflects the future goals. This helps to refine the vision so that it is simple, explicit and relevant to the individual or the organization.

Don't underestimate the power of connection and relation-ship. God may bring some strategic people into your life who will be instrumental in the formation and successful accom-plishment of the vision. Pastors, mentors, relatives, financiers, prayer intercessors, peers, helpers, teachers, and friends can all encourage you to move forward into your goal. These relation-ships should be valued, nurtured and sustained.

Identify people in your life who will matter the most in pursuit of your destiny. Some people may actually help you to discover your calling if they have observed you over a long time. They may be able to recognize what you are created to achieve and what your future could look like. Those who want to invest in your life will inspire and motivate you. If they are aware of your limitations, they may also consider how to complement you in the course of carrying out your vision.

God in His sovereignty may permit our enemies to work against us, trying to hinder us from achieving the vision. But the story of Joseph shows us that God is able to turn negative circumstances to positive ones (Genesis 50:20). He can allow unfavorable situations to work for good, for those who love Him and are called according to His purposes (Romans 8:28). While Joseph's brothers tried to stop him, they were unknowingly pushing him forward to the place where his dream was going to be realized. The evil they did turned out to be part of the fulfillment of God's plan for Joseph.

Your enemies may in fact be helping you without knowing it. Generally, we pray more fervently when we are facing difficult situations in life. It's when we feel we have come to the end of the road that we realize our need of God and become more intimate with Him. And often, the more time we spend in prayer, the sooner our answers are provided.

Personalized or particular

Any individual's vision should be personal to them. Any organizational vision should be specific to that organization, not generalized. The vision should single you or the organization out from the rest in a conspicuous way. A vision should describe your future so succinctly that when people come across your mission statements, immediately your name or that of your organization should cross their minds.

Your life is characterized by many diverse aspects including your upbringing, educational background, experience, temperament, talents, strengths and weaknesses that have characterized your life different from anyone else. You are not just the same as anyone else, so don't be tempted to formulate your vision to imitate that of others.

Identify what is uniquely your essence. Discover why you were born and what your purpose is. God created you unique and so your special assignment in life is precisely fitted to who you are. Discover exactly what the intent of God for your life is and that will enable you to live a fulfilled, productive and enjoyable life.

> Discover why you were born
> and that is your essence.

Practical

The vision should be feasible so that it can certainly come to pass. Habakkuk 2:2–3 says that the vision will come to pass and even if it delays, wait for it.

The vision must not be just a pipe-dream but something that can and will be done. It should move from theory to reality, from dream to substance. It must not be an imaginary or unrealistic expectation. In the acronym "SMART," the letters A and R stand for Achievable and Realistic. The vision is a matter of faith, but that is not the same as being presumptuous or over-ambitious. It should be achievable even if it involves stretching resources and efforts.

Passionate

A vision has to provide passion and inspiration for the visionary. This is what will supply the energy, endurance and persever-ance to take the risks and make the sacrifices needed to achieve the vision. If a person loses interest in their vision, perhaps because they are distracted by too many other things, the vision will be weakened.

A vision should preoccupy your mind. It must captivate and

stir the whole of your being. It should fill you with zeal, motivation and high level of desire, as each activity is viewed as a step closer to your destiny. A vision should excite you and generate a high interest in anything linked to it.

Published

It is very helpful if a vision is clearly written down so that it can be readily available for distribution to interested persons. Both new and old members of a church or organization need to study the document to know where they are supposed to be going. Even a personal vision should be written so that every time it is seen, it will remind the visionary why they exist and where they are going. This helps each person to maintain a focus on the vision.

Written mission statements are essential in marketing as this quickly brings the message across to the potential target group. For organizations, this may be on letterheads, brochures, business cards, even billboards.

It's biblical! The prophet Habakkuk was told by God:

> "Write down the vision, inscribe it on tablets, ready for a herald to carry it with speed; for there is still a vision for an appointed time."
>
> (Habakkuk 2:2–3, NEB)

Raising Support for the Vision

To realize a vision, resources will need to be mobilized and budgeted for. Whether the vision is personal or corporate, it will have cost implications which must be planned for. Leaders therefore must be able to guide their organization financially.

Any budget should be based on the activities linked to the objectives, which in turn relate to the overall vision. Without "activity-based budgeting," finances can easily be misplaced. It is not good practice merely to fix a percentage of the previous income and expenditure of an organization to come up with the new year's budget. It is sensible to make reference to the previous budget but the new activities and quantity of work need to be considered.

A budget is not just about what you expect to spend, but about where you will obtain the finances from. It costs money to raise money! So staff remuneration, marketing, advertising and fundraising events all need to be budgeted for. A good budget should guide the allocation of resources as well as the exercise of discipline in financial management.

There is no point in preparing a budget if it is not used. A budget is a tool to get financial results, not just to meet donor demands or stakeholders' interests. To assist in the smooth running of the organization, it needs to be formulated carefully.

A budget is just a plan and therefore changes in the costs of certain resources or services at the time of operation will affect the real costs. For non-profit organizations, it is normally not appropriate to borrow money if it will incur high interest and transaction costs. If not enough money is raised for a particular activity, it may be necessary to scale down activities or seek out more cost-effective alternatives.

A good financial management policy should guide approval systems, record keeping, and safekeeping of money, signatories and accountability. This useful tool should show who is responsible for the movement of finances. Jenny Reid says that "financial accountability, internal controls, record keeping, audit, cash flow management and financial reporting"[1] are needed for effective financial management in non-profit organizations.

Keeping to core principles

An organization should consider setting guidelines on sources of income based on its core religious, ethical and moral principles. These should also address the methodology of fundraising or resource solicitation. This will mean having to say no to funds from sources which do not reflect the integrity of the organization. Beware of distorting facts about your project to justify it to supporting organizations, and remember that the driving force of your organization should be to help those in greatest need, in the most ethical way.

Accepting supply-driven funds for administrative and office overheads can sometimes lead to losing managerial autonomy. Some donors' grants have strings attached that could tempt you to abandon core activities for new projects unrelated to your overall mission. Therefore, carefully check the terms and conditions placed on you as the recipient before impulsively accepting such provision.

Putting new administrative systems into place to satisfy donors may put pressure on untrained staff, which can also have negative cost implications. When there are multiple donors, staff will have to meet different requirements for managing and reporting finances. If these demands become too complex, it will affect overall efficiency and performance. On the other hand, it may provide an opportunity for growth and internal capacity development.

To cut down on administrative costs, non-profit organizations may benefit from using volunteer staff as much as possible. Volunteers may value the opportunity to gain experience and skills as well as the satisfaction of providing a service to the community. Occasional staff can be attached to specific project cycles to avoid having to hire full-time staff. People will only want to make this kind of contribution if they see that the vision and the mission statements of the organization are compatible with their own.

As part of the strategy for raising funds, you need public exposure, which may come through becoming aligned to a compatible corporate vision. This may offer training, mentoring or discipleship to maintain integrity.

Often the vision may require more resources than you can currently afford. This means that you need to boost your earnings so that you have adequate means to take you to your destiny. Many people can manage to do other jobs well if they stretch themselves. Earning extra income may involve spending time after hours running extra businesses, writing, or consulting. You may also need to discipline yourself to regularly save a proportion of your salary to go towards your vision.

Using leverage

Every vision requires a clear strategy for resource mobilization. To do this effectively, organizational capabilities, challenges, strengths and weaknesses should all be assessed. Each organization should identify leverages, areas of competency that can be used to solicit resources for the vision. A good fundraiser will use the people he or she knows to obtain what is needed from people he or she does not yet know. A lever is a spring to your organization. Leveraging involves utilizing one's comparative advantages skillfully in order to pull in the needed resources for the organization.

Many people have friends and partners who are willing to support their vision. Leverage means making use of these relationships to find additional support from new people and organizations. Often you can get resources that you need for your vision from people you do not yet have contact with, through the recommendations of those that you already know.

Leverage can also mean taking advantage of your current areas of competency to mobilize resources from new donors or funding agencies. To successfully gain new support, remember these leveraging techniques:

- Your reputation is built by accountability, consistency and trustworthiness in the management of the project and resources. New donors will be more ready to give additional resources if they see your integrity.
- Publicity through radio, television and the press can attract potential donors. The media tends to look for features that gain public attention, good as well as bad – so take care!
- Your financial reports should show that you are handling your budget competently. The Bible says that if you have been faithful over a little, you can be entrusted with much more (Luke 19:17). This is the principle of scaling up. Supporters will only want to increase grants or donations for projects that are being managed well.
- Donations from multilateral funding agencies will help to boost your organization's image. By showing that you have the expertise to comply with funding criteria, make project proposals and manage complex administrative systems, you may be able to access funding from other sources.

- Well-qualified and experienced staff will give potential funding sources confidence that your organization has human resources capable of implementing your planned program. External consultancy and technical support can help with specific projects, but sometimes the experience gained does not remain within the organization.
- Reports can provide critical leverage for funding. Annual reports, evaluations, strategic planning reports and financial audits of programs implemented by the organization can demonstrate your performance and technical competence.
- Vision is an essential marketing tool. Your vision and mission statements, showing why you exist and what you seek to accomplish, will cause donors to want to identify with you or your organization. This is particularly crucial for charities working for the poor and underprivileged. Remember, though, that the vision can repel certain funding sources while at the same time attracting others.

> Leveraging involves getting what you want
> from people you do not know,
> through those you know.

Why people give

Before formulating an effective strategy for raising funds or resources, it is important to know what motivates people to give. Primarily, people give to a cause or a vision that they can identify with. Having a clear vision of the organization is what will cause the flow of funds or resources to be released. There are needs all around us, but what moves people to give to one and not the other is the vision.

Some people give because of compassion for those affected by problems or catastrophes. Others do so out of obedience to

God, or see works of charity as an essential religious practice. However, charitable giving should not be manipulative or controlling, making conversion a pre-condition of receiving assistance. It is better for recipients to have the free choice to turn to faith as they see practical expressions of God's love.

Some people may give for wrong motives such as to show off or receive public praise. This is fostered by some churches which invite public pledges of money, calling people to stand in front of the congregation. This attracts people who just want to receive public recognition, even if they have no attachment to the cause. Others may pledge out of fear of embarrassment if they did not. These are not appropriate methods of fundraising. Mature believers will want to give without being paraded before others and many will opt to remain anonymous in spite of the size of their gifts.

Some givers are motivated by economic gain obtained through good publicity or tax concessions. In certain countries, charitable donations can bring substantial tax deductions. Philanthropic activity can also be a good marketing ploy, so that what a company donates is offset by the increase in sales volume and the number of clients they would eventually attract. In some cases there is political mileage in giving, and it can be used especially with poor or marginalized groups to get support in elections.

Other people give because they have more than they need, and instead of hoarding want to share their surplus resources with those who can benefit from them. God may bless some people financially in order to use them as channels of blessing to others in need.

> In fundraising, focusing on finances before relationship is being "dollar-centric."

Remember that many people give because of relationships, not just to respond to good project proposals. Focusing on finances before relationships is "dollar-centric" and does not build people and organizations. If there is a high turnover of fundraising staff, it is a signal of things not going well and organizational credibility may be lost.

When conducting fundraising events, the focus should not be solely on the amount of money to be raised, although that is important. Many non-economic benefits can be gained from a fundraising event, such as building relationships upon which future long-term funding may be built. Long-term partnerships are essential for continued and sustained support for the vision. Raising friends is more sustainable than raising funds.

Note

1. Reid, Jenny, *Seven Fundamentals for Effective Financial Management* (Cape Town, 2003), p. 2.

The Effects of a Vision

A vision has a tremendous effect on your way of life, and therefore it is bound to affect those surrounding you, whether directly or indirectly. The biblical account of Joseph shows that his dreams greatly offended his brothers and parents, who tried to resist him. Here are some inevitable effects of pursuing a vision:

The vision may strain social relationships

A vision has power to split relationships and social ties. It may cause the breaking up of some alliances and lead to the formation of new ones. In Genesis 37, we see that Joseph's dream caused conflict with those who saw themselves as objects and not beneficiaries of the vision. They were short-sighted, only seeing the negative side and failing to foresee future benefits.

Out of envy, Joseph's eleven brothers tried to prevent the realization of the dream by plotting to kill him. They were all the more resentful because of the favor his father had shown Joseph. His parents too were disturbed by the notion of bowing to him. So often, dreams of greatness don't make sense when they are revealed to very young people, especially those not on the line of inheritance to the throne, so to speak.

This is because a vision is a picture of the future which may greatly contrast with your current situation. Observers who do not share your conviction may find what you are visualizing meaningless until they see its manifestation.

Some people will not support you until they begin to see the results of your vision; they won't believe until they see. This means that a visionary's path may be lonely, having to face criticism and isolation in the initial stages. A vision has the potential to slide a wedge between closely related people. Don't be surprised if you are alienated from some people, while being attracted to others of like mind.

Accepting the vision may cause pain in some relationships while creating a great joy in others. Its radical nature may lead you to withdraw from some people, places and associations.

> A vision will attract opposition as well as support.
> It will create and reveal friends as well as foes.

A vision will attract opposition as well as support. It will create – or more precisely, reveal – enemies as well as friends. Some people will not agree with what they perceive to be unrealistic dreams and may seek to resist your efforts to get to your destiny. Others may oppose your vision because they feel jealous that you are going to become what they won't. There may be a sense of competition. Yet others who trust you will stand by and support you in the realization of your vision.

Your vision will influence what people you get close to and associate with

It will determine the type of personalities you identify with. A vision will affect who your friends are and who you bring into your inner circle.

Losing some people will be inevitable when you have a clear vision for your life. Some friendships will have to drop off; you need enough room to move forward. Ask yourself whether they are the kind of people who will contribute to your vision or those the vision will affect – your target group.

As a visionary, you should expect to attract some people and repel others. You too will be attracted to some people and be repelled by others. This is inevitable if the vision is to survive. Some will hate you and others feel a strong affinity which causes them to come on board.

Your vision will influence your choice of a spouse

Your vision will certainly have a bearing on your choice of husband or wife. If you are still single, you should think about marriage with your future in mind. Your choice of spouse should be compatible with the kind of person you are being groomed to become. A person who only fits into your current lifestyle but fails to relate to your vision can become a hindrance in your life.

Because pursuing your vision will transform you into a very different person, you cannot just consider the present moment. For a lifelong relationship such as marriage, you do not want to make decisions without taking into account your future destination. This will prevent major shipwreck in your marriage and vision. In the early stages you may only have a little idea of what your vision will develop into, but it is still vital to openly share this with your future partner.

Bear in mind the warning in Amos 3:3 that, "Do two walk together unless they have agreed to do so?" (NIV). Some people may not stay with you for long on your journey because they are going somewhere else. To end up at the same destination, you need to be in unity.

Your vision will influence your business partnerships

Your vision should also influence the kind of business partnerships that you establish. In making a business and investment decisions, take care to consider the personal vision of the prospective partner so that any differences that may cause a conflict later can be resolved earlier. Some differences may be so serious that you do not get into the partnership at all.

Ask yourself whether the person has similar goals and purposes to yours. If there are no areas of convergence, you may be courting danger and conflict may show up later. This could be costly in terms of lawsuits and mediation expenses, and may affect your corporate reputation or personal integrity.

The fact that both of you are Christians is not sufficient ground on its own for business harmony. There have been numerous cases where believers have failed to run businesses together. Take enough time and seek to make a well-informed decision in line with the will of God. If you make the right decision, it will pay dividends – you will not regret waiting.

The vision may cause displacement

To fulfill a vision, the person that God is calling may well need to move geographically. The vision may be given in one place and yet be fulfilled in another locality, which calls for sacrifice and patience. Because of a vision, you may decide to resign your current job or change your career altogether. A vision will re-align your whole life.

Abraham was called from his community of Haran to a distant place. He had to leave the rest of his family in order to be where God had planned him to be. This kind of move may appear unnatural and unreasonable to other people. We need a long-term perspective to understand the nature of a vision and to tolerate the time needed for its accomplishment.

Many Christians who chose to respond to God's call for missionary work in far countries had problems getting the full support of their family members. William Carey's wife Dorothy resisted her husband's call to India and did not want to accompany him when he left in 1793. Carey's church also found it hard to accept that the pastor who had built them up spiritually should leave them and his family behind. Yet he did this out of love for his Lord, saying, "Expect great things from God; attempt great things for God." [1]

The unfavorable situations that Joseph found himself in may have caused him to fear that his dreams would never be fulfilled. Being forcibly removed to a foreign country and later thrown in jail appeared to distance him from the realization of his vision, but actually took him nearer to its fulfillment. Each setback was only a short-term detour.

At the appointed time, Joseph walked to freedom, moving from prison to palace. What a glorious moment that was. His journey was not an easy one, but the dream of his life finally came true. Likewise, our journey to fulfill our vision may not be easy and straightforward. We may face unique problems to be solved, battles to be fought and delays that stretch our patience.

Joseph was physically displaced as God took him far from Israel to be raised up as second in command in the Egyptian government. His journey teaches us that many obstacles may have to be endured before arriving at our final destiny but we should not give up our dreams out of frustration. We need to persevere, knowing that at the right time, our vision will come to fruition.

Remember that the destiny Jesus Christ carried for the redemption of humanity caused Him to leave heaven and come to the earth. We should not be surprised if the fulfillment of our vision also leads us to relocate to new places. Prepare to move, as it may be the perfect arrangement of God for your life.

Your vision will influence your choices

A true vision should cause you to become selective about the choices you make in your life. You won't just take any job you are offered, you won't just marry anybody who comes along, and you won't just live anywhere. A vision should compel you to do certain things and not others. It should preoccupy your mind and heart so that the decisions you make are based on strong convictions about the purpose of your life. This should not, however, cause you to make outrageous demands for selfish gain.

When you have a vision, your primary focus is to nourish and support it. You won't have to attend every conference, you won't have to accept every invitation, you won't have to read any book that is printed, and you won't have to associate with everybody just for the sake of it. I have come across a number of leaders who are on the move all the time, spending more than half of their pastoral time attending conferences, seminars and meetings that produce little or no change in their ministries. Not all meetings are for you, although they may be for someone else. If they are not the ones you should be attending, they will be time wasters in your life.

A vision will cause you to make radical decisions based on your convictions. A visionary must exercise restraint with non-productive activities and associations. There will always be distractions in life to slow your progress, but you don't want to spend critical resources going in circles. Focus on your agenda. The way you conduct your day-to-day activities has to line up with the strategies for fulfilling your vision. Learn to say "No!" because you know what matters the most.

Your vision will influence your time management

The vision will influence the way you use your time. Your time management reveals what is in your heart. When you have a vision, you value time as a critical resource because you aim at accomplishing each activity within a specified time frame.

Be mindful that there is a time for everything under the sun (Ecclesiastes 3:1–10). Knowing what to do within each season is important in causing the vision to flourish or else it will wither. No vision is for an indefinite period; we are not on this earth for eternity. Each vision has a time to start and a time for completion.

As someone carrying a vision, you do not have time to do everything. You will have time for some things and not for others.

> When you have a vision,
> you won't have time for everything.
> Only people without a vision
> have the time for anything.

Everyone has the same number of hours per day and yet some people are far more productive and successful than others. This is a clear indication of how the management of time differs between people. It is often said, "If you need something done, look for a busy person to do it" because of the way that such people manage their time.

In the "two-thirds world" countries, especially black Africa, management of time is so lax that hardly anyone expects meetings to start at the stipulated time. "Meetings begin when the last person arrives and end when the last person leaves"[2] and this is justified by the saying, "timing is more important than the time." But this African attitude shows a lack of value for time, and causes us to be relatively unproductive.

In some charismatic meetings, leaders call their lack of discipline in managing time the "leading of the Spirit." They may be so event-oriented that as long as everybody seems to be enjoying the event, they keep going, only closing the meeting when interest is beginning to decline. This is a major contrast with the way that God manages time.

Although God lives outside of time, He does seriously keep the time. The entire creation was completed on schedule with specific times and days for each task. There was a night and a day after each work of creation. Jesus came in the *fullness of time*. When God spoke about visiting His people, we often see it recorded as "this time next year, at the appointed time." In referring to death, the Bible says, "It is appointed [i.e. a time is set aside] for men to die once" (Hebrews 9:27, NASB). Events happened and ended at a certain predetermined time. Jesus could not be arrested until His time "had come."

When you are a person of destiny, time is a very important resource. Critical opportunities may be lost through unproductive activities or by taking more time than necessary in doing something. The Lord warned the Israelites that they had overstayed at Mount Horeb and that it was time for them to break camp and move on (Deuteronomy 1:6). The Bible encourages believers to "walk circumspectly, not as fools, but as wise, redeeming the time, because the days are evil" (Ephesians 5:15, KJV). Effective time management will increase your productivity.

You need to be at certain places for specific lengths of time if you are to achieve the best results. This should not be compromised if you want to keep focused. Do not allow yourself to be distracted from your vision by time-wasting relationships, unproductive meetings and associations. Count the cost by putting value on time. Never mark time, like soldiers who are just marching in place. Ensure that the energy you exert pushes you forward.

Your vision will affect your financial discipline

The next issue of vital importance is your financial management. Where do you invest your monetary resources? Your vision should take a significant share of your earnings. The activities that you do to pursue your dream will demand financial commitment; each portion of your strategy must be budgeted for. You have to be willing to spend time and money to nourish your dream and not fritter it away on non-essentials.

Your vision will determine where your treasure goes. To cause your vision to flourish, you may need to invest in books, magazines, subscriptions, memberships or club affiliations. It may also be necessary to attend certain meetings or courses. Never stop learning new things that will be beneficial for the development of your vision.

> Your vision will determine where most of your treasure is and where it goes.

The vision will influence your organizational culture

A corporate vision must influence the culture adopted by the organization. Titles, symbols, policies, procedures, norms and values that govern the organization all reflect its personality and show how things are being done in the organization. The culture of the organization should not set the vision, but rather, the vision should influence the culture. First determine how the vision will be achieved, then establish the culture to support it. If the culture of the organization does not suit the vision, it may be difficult to achieve the vision with it.

Titles can mean a lot to some people and little or nothing to others. In practice, roles, responsibilities and service are more important than titles. Servant leadership is not about what title you hold but what service you do. The function and the responsibilities of a person are the most important thing. In the Bible, the emphasis is not on titles but on servanthood and being doers of the Word.

Your vision will energize you to perform above average

To accomplish extraordinary things, your performance needs to be out of the ordinary. Minimum effort will only achieve average performance. But dedication to your vision will provide the energy needed to persevere, endure and make sacrifices that move you forward.

The positive forces that foster your vision need to be strong to counter the negative forces that impede your forward motion. In force field analysis (see p. 53), these different forces are called sustaining and restraining forces respectively.

Carrying a vision is like carrying a pregnancy. It means being singled out to achieve a very special task. You will need to develop certain routines that someone else might find laborious, meaningless or impossible to do. Other habits will need to be broken in order to concentrate on the ones that foster the vision.

A vision calls for accountability

In order to succeed in implementing your vision, you need to be accountable to others. If you refuse to be answerable for your decisions and actions, a lack of checks and balances can lead to shipwreck of your life and vision. Accountability is about submission to another person who holds you responsible for your activities and also your motives.

There are several directions of accountability. Accountability should be upward – to God, to superiors, to leadership, to the board and to the mentor. Every visionary needs a good mentor to provide guidance that prevents them from going astray. In horizontal accountability, you look to friends or peer mentors, while in a downward relationship (less essential) you look to followers, disciples or mentorees.

There will be no true accountability in a corporate situation if issues of control and shared responsibilities are not addressed. Accountability is not just reporting – anyone can produce paperwork or make a statement. It is shown in people's willingness to be questioned about their decisions and actions without taking offence. Accountability should be seen in terms of the trust fostered through delegation, shared decision-making and the level of participation and teamwork by leaders.

Without an open and vulnerable organizational culture, there can be no true accountability. Leaders need to believe in others and involve them in doing work that is proportional to their abilities, even if it means having to apply more effort to reach set targets. Accountability also involves listening to people without suspicion. Team ministry should allow for ever-wider participation of others in the implementation of the vision.

Too much burden on the shoulders of one person creates a work overload and may result in burnout. Moses nearly experienced this problem until his father in-law Jethro advised him to start delegating the leadership. Breaking up the work-load into various manageable blocks eases administration and facilitates dealing with various issues.

Sometimes there is an opposite problem when an individual is overqualified for their tasks and experiences work "under-load." Such a person will feel frustrated and unfulfilled as work becomes monotonous and a mere routine. Low-level performers may not mind this situation, but a high rate of staff turnover can indicate that middle and higher performers may be looking for more challenging opportunities elsewhere.

Certain leaders refuse to let go of activities meant for more junior staff because of their own sense of insecurity. They feel they must be constantly busy and appear indispensable. For others, it is more to do with pride and the question of who takes the glory when the job is done well. If all results are attributed to their personal efforts and there is little recognition of the other members of the team, this substantially reduces the effect-iveness of the organization.

When success of an organization is attributed only to the leader rather than to the team, there is a failure to understand the corporate identity of the vision. Some leaders over-emphasize their own personality, as if the vision was not owned by the whole organization. This causes frustration among the staff who feel like mere hired staff to do the work for the visionary.

With a corporate vision, there is no majority shareholding. Each person has a proportion of the bigger vision, whether minor or major. The metaphor of the body in Scripture shows that all are important, notwithstanding the relative sizes of the individual parts. Measuring the input of individuals in an organization can make them feel inferior and unwanted. It can be a major reason for people leaving in search of other opportunities where they feel their contributions will be more appreciated.

Notes

1. Finnie, Kellsye M., *William Carey, by Trade a Cobbler* (Eastbourne: Kingsway Publications, 1986), p. 47.
2. Lingenfelter, S.G. and Mayers, M.K., *Ministering Cross-Culturally* (Grand Rapids: Baker Book House, 1998), p. 42.

Overcoming Threats to a Vision

We turn to the crucial issue of threats to a vision's fulfillment. Can a vision actually die because of attacks against it? Some people believe that when a vision dies, it can be brought to life again. Others believe that when a dream dies, you can dream another dream. The question I would like to pose here is, can a vision actually die or fail completely? Can a vision be prevented from being fulfilled?

First, it is important to remember that a vision is something God has destined for your life or your organization. He has planned something very specific for your future. If God provides the vision, can He yet allow it to die? Why would He permit that?

Although a vision is God's will and plan, the responsibility for performing it does not completely rest on Him. There is both a divine and human side to achieving the vision. We have to work out the process of achieving that dream with the help of God.

It is people who fall into temptations that threaten their dreams, not God. When Joseph was tempted by his master's wife, he had to personally resist and run away from sin. When we face temptation we need to use the routes of escape that God has provided. If Joseph did not resist the blandishments of Potiphar's wife, his dream would have been frustrated and utterly destroyed.

God will not force a vision to be accomplished by any person.
When Adam and Eve were tempted in the Garden of Eden,
they chose to turn away from His will for them. There has to be
a personal willingness and cooperation with God so that the
dream can be realized. If we persevere through attacks and
delays, the dream will always be sustained. As long as we are
faithful, God will accomplish His part, because He cannot fail.

> At the destined hour, it will come in breathless haste,
> it will not fail.
> If it delays, wait for it;
> for when it comes will be no time to linger.
>
> (Habakkuk 2:3, NEB)

When you fall in the midst of the race, stand up and start
running again. You can fall seven times and yet be able to rise
up again. Don't just lie on the ground but be determined to stay
in the race.

God is fully in control over human affairs and nothing can
happen outside of His permission. You can be sure that He is
fully aware of what is happening in your life. He may allow
certain things to happen without necessarily having initiated
them. God will use the trying circumstances in our lives to
strengthen our faith.

When your vision is from God, He will do His part to
support it until it is fulfilled. What He says He will do, and
whatever He has ordained will certainly happen.

> God who gives the vision also sustains
> both the vision as well as the visionary.

If the vision appears to die, God can cause it to be
resurrected. What we need is not another dream but the same
God-given dream re-activated, re-aligned, restored and directed
to the end. There are always enemies or obstacles that work

against the vision, but the Bible says, "No weapon that is formed against you will prosper" (Isaiah 54:17, NASB). This gives us security because we know that, "[God] who began a good work in you will carry it on to completion" (Philippians 1:6, NIV).

Enemies can fight our vision. We see that Jesus Christ's destiny was resisted when people plotted to have Him killed prematurely. They failed because Jesus was not meant to die any other death than the one planned by God, on the cross for the atonement of our sins.

Pharaoh decreed that all Israelite babies should be put to death. The midwives could have killed Moses but he was preserved and lived to receive a vision for his life. Because of that vision the children of Israel were liberated from their 430 years of captivity in Egypt.

We have already seen that Joseph's dream was resisted and his brothers conspired to kill him. Many other events conspired to stop the vision from coming to fruition but thank God, all things worked together for good in that what the brothers meant for evil, God turned out for good. Even prison was an opportunity for his divine skills of interpreting dreams to be made known. Joseph's vision survived and finally all the details were fulfilled just as in his dream. This was possible because he persevered in righteousness and the fear of God. Any failure on his part could have rendered his dream unattainable.

In these examples we see that despite opposition, every dream that came from God eventually succeeded because the hand of God was upon the visionaries' lives to keep them through to the very end. Jesus, Moses and Joseph were all obedient and the result was the fulfillment of their God-ordained visions.

Threats to children of destiny

We see a number of people in the Bible who were promised children by God, but before the child of promise was born, the devil tried to stop the conception. Women were attacked with barrenness as they were scheduled to carry children of great destinies. Think about these biblical examples:

- Sarah was barren and way past the age of childbearing, despite God's promise that the child would be born through her. Later Isaac was born, a name that means "laughter" or "great joy." God made it possible in spite of what seemed like insuperable obstacles.
- Hannah cried before the Lord in the temple because she could not conceive a child. She did not give up and Samuel was born in answer to prayer, later to become a great prophet of God.
- The wife of Manoah was also barren but after her vow to God, Samson was born from her womb. Samson means "strong to deliver." He single-handedly fought the Philistines because of the unique anointing that was upon his life. Even in his death, Samson killed large numbers of Philistines.
- Elizabeth was too old to bear any child, but out of her barren womb came John the Baptist, the great forerunner of Jesus Christ.

In spite of the devil's efforts to stop the purposes of God by closing the wombs of these women, the power of God ultimately prevailed. God will always bring His plans for His people to birth. Therefore, if the dream you are carrying is of God, no amount of resistance by the forces of hell can stop what the Lord has planned.

That does not mean that you should be complacent in your Christian walk. In fact, the more genuine the vision is, the more certain it is that there will be attempts to stop or hinder it from being accomplished. Therefore, as carriers of a vision, we need to be alert to attacks and obstacles that may hinder our focus on the goal.

The sustainability of the vision depends on both God and the visionary playing their essential parts. If the visionary falls into sin, their part in the vision may be affected but ultimately God will still achieve His divine goal. God can do without us but we cannot without Him.

Let us look at threats to the vision which we need to avoid or resist.

Challenge from counterfeit visions

A counterfeit vision is a condition so similar to the vision that it is mistaken for the real thing. It can deceive you into thinking you have arrived at the final destination when you are not. Counterfeits offer partial fulfillment and satisfaction, but the results are not what you are really seeking. When you clearly understand your vision, you will know that there is yet more to achieve than what you see.

After you have spent a long time looking at the vision, the counterfeits will be easily distinguished. No matter how appealing the dummies look, the journey needs to continue. When you arrive at your vision's fulfillment, the signs will be evident!

Envy

There is a remarkable story in the Bible about David's return from the battle against Goliath and the Philistines. Women were singing David's praises and it angered King Saul to be compared unfavorably with the younger, untrained soldier David.

Jealousy was King Saul's greatest problem and he began to perceive a threat to his royal position. He feared that David would capitalize on his popularity to overthrow him and was terribly embittered. Perhaps the embittered Saul reasoned that if David could kill Goliath, he could kill anyone else.

Jealousy may come from those above you who feel threatened by your competence, for fear that you may try to take over their position or that they may lose influence and control.

They may fear the loss of privileges such as transport, housing, office, wages, etc. Yet when people are secure in their calling, they have no need for envy or jealousy. The success of an individual should be viewed as the success of the group – as was the case with David's victory, which benefited the entire nation of Israel.

Jealousy can come from peers who think that you don't deserve a certain destiny because others appear to be better qualified to be promoted. Your vision can be a major threat to people who do not value your dream and may want to frustrate you from achieving it.

When Jesse was asked to parade his sons before the prophet Samuel so that he could anoint one from among them as king over Israel, he only considered some suitable for presenting. David was not selected by his father for consideration, but the young boy was the one upon whom the hand of God was resting.

God will always ensure that His will comes to pass. The Bible speaks of Jesus being the stone the builders rejected who then became the Chief Cornerstone. What men reject, God may select and place in strategic positions.

Competition

In organizations, jealousy can come from competitors who are fighting for the same market share, audience or clientele. Unfortunately Christians can also struggle unnecessary comparisons such as who is the pastor of the biggest church or the fastest growing ministry, who commands the biggest annual budget, the largest workforce, or who drives the most powerful vehicle.

God will always supply provisions that are commensurate with the size of the vision. But these resources are not a measure of success, and should not be treated as an end in themselves. It is the source of the provisions that are important, not the size of them. Success should be measured in terms of the extent to which they contribute to achieving the vision.

In working at your vision, avoid being drawn into the worldly spirit of competition. You have your own race to run and your own dream to account for. If it is from God (as it should always be) then rest assured that you will have all that is needed to get through. If you shift your focus from looking to the goal to looking at what's happening around you, you will be distracted from the vision.

Hurrying the vision

One thing that can lead to aborted dreams is a premature launch into the ministry. The Word of God clearly states that there is an appointed, or set, time at which a vision will be realized. This means that the vision should be allowed to go through its full gestation period before it is launched.

People should always guard against a premature response to prophecies. Prophetic words can tell of events that are to happen very soon as well as those that will take place in centuries to come. The fact that someone prophesies that you will be in a leadership role does not mean that you will get enthroned within the next twenty-four hours! Patient preparation is needed before you become capable of handling the fully manifested vision.

> Each vision is for an appointed time.

There is a time for each vision to come to birth. When the "pregnancy" has come to full term, it is time for delivery. Overexcitement, impatience and immaturity can cause people to push forward the birth of their vision and miss God's timing.

Procrastination – not now, but later

Procrastination is the enemy of the present. It makes you feel that there is still more time ahead to do this or that. You postpone the critical activities that would help you realize your dream to a later date, next week, next month and years ahead.

A vision just doesn't fit into any period of time; it is for an appointed time. This time is fixed so that the vision will be fulfilled at exactly the right moment to bless the individual, organization or society.

It is also true that one vision may be an essential link for another vision to be achieved. If one vision is delayed then the associated vision will equally fall out of schedule. Think of how critical the prompt obedience of Mary the mother of Jesus Christ was in terms of the plan of salvation.

Whatever vision you have, it will be linked to the life of another person or organization. Your faithfulness in fulfilling your destiny will affect the destiny of other people. Divine providence ensures that there is grace to sustain every godly vision and to protect your life, so allow your vision to fit into God's timing and do not do later what you are supposed to do now.

Sometimes people procrastinate because the current conditions don't seem to match the requirements of the vision. Yet you will never know that the water will hold you unless you step out of the boat in faith. Implementing a vision is an act of faith.

Vision deviations

Deviations from the vision are the things that lead away from the right direction. The detour may be only temporary, in which case you can come back to the main road. If this deviation is permanent, then you have gone completely astray.

Deviations can be caused by pressure for survival, such as a desire to raise money to support the family which may lead you into doing something that is not directly related to the vision. It may be peer pressure if you are influenced by seeing what others appear to be accomplishing more successfully.

If you have not yet become aware of your vision, you can be misled by the temporal satisfaction of your job or business. Sometimes, prior experiences, expertise and relationships can be used in leverage to enhance the vision. Yet remember that the devil tempted Jesus with a portion of the Kingdom if He was prepared to worship him. When temptations come, focus on the Word of God and keep your vision on the rails.

Enemies

Every vision has its enemies, but the type of resistance is unique to each situation. Obstacles can rise up at the time the vision is made public, perhaps old foes who contend to stop or frustrate your vision. We have said earlier that a vision attracts both friends as well as foes, and you need to know how to manage both.

A vision is an attractive prospect, so opposition to it is a sign that others may want something good that they see you have. If out of jealousy they try to frustrate its fulfillment, it signifies that it is something precious and worth fighting for.

> To every seed, there is a specific weed.

Hypocrites are people who pretend that they are on your side but only want to steal your ideas, hijack the vision and rob you of your great investment and opportunity. They associate with you only enough to get what they want, not to make a worthwhile contribution to your vision. They are deceivers.

Delilah was a typical hypocrite. She pretended to be a friend of Samson but was acting deceitfully. She had been promised a large reward by the Philistine army commanders to spy on Samson and trick him into revealing the secret of his anointing, so that they could torture and destroy him.

Negative circumstances

Negative events in our lives tend to be interpreted as obstacles, yet the Bible tells us, "all things work together for good to those who love God, to those who are called according to His purpose" (Romans 8:28, NASB). It is hard to see any redemptive purpose in apparently evil circumstances when we are in the midst of them, but sometimes our eyes open up when we reach the end of the road. When we look back on the journey, we can appreciate that even in the dark moments of our lives, God was working on our side and for our good.

These negative circumstances can enable us to experience God's saving grace. Problems often bring us into contact with new people whom we would not have met otherwise, and they stretch our faith. Problems can make us pray more than we could have done if we had no challenges. We are often unhappy at the time of testing, but joy does come when we remain faithful in times of affliction and finally triumph over evil.

Such encounters may be the door to our destiny. They provide opportunities for experiencing God's providence to a degree that we would not have known without those apparent problems.

The fear that Moses was going to be killed forced his mother to hide him in a basket on the water. This resulted in the baby being taken in to be part of the royal family and receiving the privileges of diet, education, care and upbringing like any king's child. Moses would not have experienced this if not for those unfavorable circumstances, and through this came redemption for the whole nation of Israel.

In Joseph's situation, his brothers' dehumanizing and rejecting acts led him to Egypt where he eventually became the Prime Minister. Moreover, the terrible torture that Christ experienced when He was nailed to the cross was actually the means of accomplishing the eternal plan for the redemption for humanity.

> Problems are pressure builders
> and when the pressure rises,
> we can rise with it.

Problems are pressure builders and when the pressure rises, we can rise with it. Even as we face the greatest opposition and our hopes seem dashed, our promotion may be near. May God help us respond to trials by using the pressure to lift us up instead of suppressing us. The obstacles may be the stepping-stones to our destiny.

Hard and unpleasant moments in our lives may be the very paths that will lead to a door of destiny later on. Consider the life of Jesus Christ, whose purpose was to atone for the sins of the whole world. By inciting false witnesses and perversion of justice by both Pilate and Herod, the devil unwittingly pushed Jesus closer to His God-ordained destiny – the cross. Although it looked like the ultimate defeat, Christ's sacrificial death brought about the redemption of souls. The devil was signing his own death warrant and lost the battle against God's saints.

Examples of threatened visions that never died

Here is a short list of dreams or visions that in spite of resistance, hindrances and opposition still got accomplished.

- Jesus was born on the earth with the purpose of redeeming humankind, but King Herod viewed the baby Jesus as a competitor for power. Like Pharaoh in the days of Moses, Herod tried to kill all the young boys in order to frustrate the plans of God. By divine providence and intervention, Jesus was spared, and later was preserved from the efforts of the High Priests to kill Him, because He had not yet fulfilled His life's purpose. In the fullness of time He died on the cross, atoning for our sins just as God had planned.

- In South Africa, Nelson Mandela's fight for the liberation of his black countrymen led to his imprisonment for twenty-seven years at Roben Island on the Indian Ocean. Despite his long incarceration, the vision which he stood for was still alive when he was released in 1989 and a racially tolerant and free nation was born.

- The civil rights activist, Martin Luther King Jr, had a dream that one day racial barriers would be broken in America. Although he was brutally assassinated in 1968, the dream still came to pass for the benefits of blacks and whites in that nation.
- We have already looked at Joseph's dream of ruling over his whole family and how he faced major resistance and opposition. Despite all the unfavorable conditions that he experienced, one day he sat on the throne before which the father and brothers knelt. It took a long time, but it came to pass.
- Again, we have seen how Moses was destined to lead the people of Israel out of their bondage in Egypt. Despite Pharoah's plan to kill all male babies, by God's sovereignty Moses' mother was attended by midwives who defied the king's orders and allowed the baby to live. After Pharaoh's daughter picked him out of the basket on the water, Moses was brought to live in the royal palace – so the same person who tried to kill him actually brought him up with all the privileges of a prince. Moses learned Egyptian law, which was essential for his task of freeing his fellow Israelites. Even when he died, Joshua was standing by as his successor to complete the task and move the people into the Promised Land. The death of the visionary is not the death of the vision if we learn to pass on the baton to another person as God directs.
- David was another extraordinary man in the Bible to whom God gave a vision. He was called, "a man after God's own heart." The book of Acts tells us that when David had accomplished the purpose of God in his generation, he died. He did not die before the purpose of God was achieved (Acts 13:36).

Jesus could not be killed before the fullness of time, because both the timing and nature of His death were pre-determined by God. Nothing could alter the plan that God had set for Jesus

Christ and the assignment He was sent to accomplish. When He was arrested, Jesus declared that "Father, the hour has come" (John 17:1, NASB), and when His momentous task on the cross was accomplished, He said, "It is finished" (John 19:30). In fact He gave up His spirit freely, saying, "Father, into Your hands I commit My spirit" (Luke 23:46, NASB).

Jesus declared that the Son of Man goes as it is written of Him, meaning that whatever happened to Him was according to God's pre-recorded plan. His life and His death were all clearly according to God's perfect time schedule. Likewise, nobody's course of life can be changed contrary to God's sovereign purpose if we remain faithful to Him.

When Paul was about to die, he declared that he had run his race and fought the good fight of faith. Completing the vision makes us ready to depart from this body. Once we cross the finishing line, we should rest.

The vision lives on

We see from these examples that the forces of darkness cannot overcome a truly God-given vision, as long as the visionary remains faithful and focused on the call. When God provides a vision to someone, He does not leave the matter of its survival to chance. He is there to support and protect it, through and through. He comes alongside and works with us.

> When God provides a vision to someone,
> He does not leave its fulfillment to chance.

Also, God will teach us how that vision will be accomplished, even though the full process may be unknown to us at the start, because "we know in part and we prophesy in part" (1 Corinthians 13:9 NIV). While God is working with us, we must remain committed to Him and be consistent in doing what He has assigned for us to do.

There are benefits in not getting the full details of our future because some of the situations we will encounter may be quite frightening – it's better to cross those bridges when we come to them. Also, we need to learn lessons about handling new situations with courage and faith, and we learn best when we face these situations.

A visionary may die but not the vision that he carries. The death of the person who conceived the vision need not lead to the death of the vision itself. The visionary's part of the vision may be completed and others will arise to carry on and complete the work. Some visionaries are pioneers who were created for just that first part of the vision, and their own work is completed as they fulfill their proportion.

We can expect to face severe resistance and opposition before our vision is fulfilled, but without losing hope of its fulfillment. Ultimately every vision satisfies God's plan for creating you or your ministry. It is to benefit God's purposes and we are actually the secondary beneficiaries.

> The visionary may die
> while the vision lives on.

We have already seen how Moses only took the Israelites as far as Mount Nebo and Joshua covered the rest of the journey into the Promised Land. The story of David is another case in point. It was his son Solomon who finally built the temple for God, even though David desired to do so.

Some visions have a bigger lifespan than the visionary. It is crucial that leaders understand that the vision can outlive the visionary, and they are not inseparable from the vision they conceive or carry. Someone else may be next on the ladder.

If you start a work, you may not necessarily be the one to complete it. Visions with a wide scope may need to be phased, so different generations do their part to contribute to the whole. So leaders must not think short-term, but understand that they may play a small but useful part in the ultimate completion of the vision.

It makes sense that bigger visions have a longer gestation period than smaller ones. So prepare yourself accordingly and avoid unnecessary haste. Do not turn a marathon into a sprint simply because you want to see the fulfillment of your vision in your generation. Align yourself with the natural timings of God. You do not need to push or manipulate anybody for the sake of quick results. God will make everything appropriate in its time (Ecclesiastes 3:11).

> The size of the vision
> is proportional to its gestation period.
> The bigger the vision, the longer it takes
> to come to birth.

Any vision should render glory to God, and not to man. The timeframe of your activities needs to be proportionate to the size of your vision. Allow enough preparation time to accomplish your dream.

It has been said:

> If you think in terms of one year, sow grain.
> If you think in terms of ten years, plant trees
> If you think in terms of one hundred years, train people.
>
> (Author unknown)

Challenges to the vision

The time between the revelation of the vision and its fulfillment is essentially the gestation period of the vision. During this phase, resistance, obstacles and challenges are encountered that threaten the progress of the vision. This is a time of great testing for the vision, and without perseverance it is possible to give up and abandon the work.

Any visionary should be braced for major encounters during this phase. Never attempt to fight the battle using human efforts, as this may be fatal. We need to depend on the power of God because the battle will not be against flesh and blood, even though the agents may be seen to be human beings.

It is for this reason that Paul urged the church at Ephesus to be strong in the Lord and in the power of His might (Ephesians 6:10). There is a stronger power on the inside of a believer than there is on the outside because He that is in us is greater than he that is in the world (1 John 4:4). You may be frail on the outside, but you are a giant on the inside because of the one who indwells you. As someone once said, "it is not the size of the dog in the fight but the size of the fight in the dog that wins the victory."

This is actually an opportunity to grow in managing the vision. During this period we must avoid being swayed from our focus, as the counter forces or internal weaknesses in the organization can cause a split vision or division (*di-vision*).

Overcoming resistance and tension

In practice, some threatening and unfavorable circumstances can actually become positive opportunities. It is important to recognize which negative situations have some hidden good in them. You may need to find strategies that are more effective in achieving the desired result. Alternative approaches may help eliminate the negative forces or potential risks, and utilize positive forces to add buoyancy to the vision.

Identifying the restraining forces is necessary before working out how to deal with resistance. Resistance should not be avoided but it should be broken through. It has been said, "Following the path of least resistance makes both men and rivers crooked."

The experience of dealing with obstacles, hindrances and threats can build confidence and courage to tackle challenges later in life. The Bible tells us that David used his early experience of fighting lions and bears to generate faith and courage to deal with Goliath later on.

A strong vision will overcome internal weaknesses, limitations and fear in your life. A person with a God-given vision cannot be overcome, slowed down, suppressed or stopped. With such a vision, you are more than a conqueror, and are already an overcomer. Temporary attacks and setbacks will come but ultimately, the resisting forces will have to give way and you, the visionary, will get to the other side of the mountain.

Bibliography

Burn, J., *Fishing for the King: Building Church to Reach the Unchurched* (New Wine Press, 1997).

Christian Leadership World, www.teal.org.uk/vl/ v13vlead.html, Internet, accessed on 18 September 2003.

Conner, K., *The Church in the New Testament* (Sovereign World, 1982).

Cormack D., *Change Directions: New Ways Forward for Your Life, Church and Business* (Crowborough: Monarch, 1995).

Dinnen, S., *You Can Learn to Lead: A Manual for People in Leadership* (Christian Focus, 1998).

Finnie, K.M., *William Carey, By Trade a Cobbler* (Eastbourne: Kingsway Publications, 1986).

Gordon, B., *The Leader's Vision*, Master Builder Series (Tonbridge: Sovereign World, 1990).

Gordon, B. and Fardouly, D., *Master Builders: Developing Life and Leadership in the Body of Christ Today* (Tonbridge: Sovereign World, 1990).

Holland, J. and Blackburn, J. *Whose Voice? Participatory Research and Policy Change* (London: Intermediate Technology Publication, 1998).

King, P., *Leadership Explosion: Maximizing Leadership Potential in the Church* (London and Sydney: Hodder and Stoughton, 1987).

Kouzes, J.M. and Posner, B.Z. *The Leadership Challenge: How to Keep Getting Extraordinary Things Done in Organizations* (San Francisco: Jossey-Bass, 1997).

Lingenfelter, S.G. and Mayers, M.K., *Ministering Cross-Culturally* (Grand Rapids: Baker Book House, 1998).

Malphurs, A., *Advanced Strategic Planning: A New Model for Church and Ministry Leaders* (Grand Rapids, Michigan: Baker Books, 1999).

Marshall, Tom, *Understanding Leadership* (Tonbridge: Sovereign World, 1991).

Perry, John, *Effective Christian Leadership* (London, Sydney and Toronto: Hodder and Stoughton, 1983).

Reid, J., *Seven Fundamentals for Effective Financial Management* (Cape Town: Juta Academic, 2003).

Shearman, D., *Born to Win: Discovering your Destiny on the Journey to the Promised Land* (Sovereign World, 1999).

Stephens, C.O., *Leading Groups in Civil Society* (White River, 1999).

Wiersbe, W., *On Being a Servant of God* (Grand Rapids, Michigan: Baker Books, 1993).

About the author

Pukuta Mwanza holds a Bachelor of Mineral Sciences degree in Metallurgy and Mineral Processing from the University of Zambia, a Master of Arts degree in Rural Social Development from the University of Reading in England and a Master of Arts degree in Organizational Leadership from Eastern University, Pennsylvania in the United States.

Pukuta is involved in preaching, training, consultancy, organizational and leadership capacity development. His book *A Christian Attitude towards Suffering and Pain* is published by Sovereign World Ltd. He is married to Maggie and they have two sons and two daughters, Chisomo, Chikondi, Pukuta Jr and Taonga.

Author's contact details:

Pukuta N. Mwanza
PO Box 33377
Lusaka 10101
Zambia
Central Africa

Email: pnmwanza@yahoo.com
Website: www.pukuta.com

We hope you enjoyed reading this Sovereign World book.
For more details of other Sovereign books and
new releases see our website:

www.sovereignworld.com

If you would like to help us send a copy of this book
and many other titles to needy pastors in developing
countries, please write for further information
or send your gift to:

Sovereign World Trust
PO Box 777
Tonbridge, Kent TN11 0ZS
United Kingdom

You can also visit **www.sovereignworldtrust.com**.
The Trust is a registered charity.